THE GREAT AMERICAN BAKE SALE

ALISON BOTELER

BARRON'S

All inquiries should be addressed to:
Barron's Educational Series, Inc.
250 Wireless Boulevard
Hauppauge, New York 11788

Library of Congress Catalog Card No. 90-47789

International Standard Book No. 0-8120-4314-6

Library of Congress Cataloging in Publication Data

Boteler, Alison Molinare.
  The great American bake sale / by Alison Boteler.
    p.   cm.
  ISBN 0-8120-4314-6
  1. Baking.   I. Title.
TX765.B67   1991
641.7′1—dc20   90-47789
                                                       CIP

Design by Milton Glaser, Inc.
Illustrations by Chi-ming Kan
Matthew Klein, photographer
Rick Ellis, food stylist
Jessica Agullo, prop stylist

PRINTED IN HONG KONG
3456 9927 9876

My Special Thanks...

To Peter and Pauline Lang, Franz and Beth Schober (and Casper, "The Country Inn Cat"), for taste-testing my many experiments.

To Jackee Mason, for putting it all together.

To Grace Freedson and Carolyn Horne, for making this book possible.

CONTENTS

INTRODUCTION

The bake sale is the backbone of America. From brownies to Mom's apple pie, bake sales are the showcase of American desserts…and where would America be without dessert?

Along with sweet treats and snacks, bake sales are the breadbasket of American culture. Bake sales bring together the best recipes of our ethnic and regional heritage, Grandmother's hand-me-downs, legendary Junior League cookbooks…and the backs of cereal boxes!

Bake sales are a bounty of brainstorms. Creative cooks across the country have used their kitchens as chemistry sets, concocting some classics: tomato soup cake, carrot cookies, even potato chip cookies. Necessity is the source of substitution—and, of course, the mother of invention. That must be why ingenious mothers invented many of our childhood treats. How else can you explain cornflake macaroons? The originator of mayonnaise pie crust was another Einstein!

This book is about all those homey, nostalgic goodies you just can't buy anywhere, except at a bake sale. It's a source of recipes that will inspire you to support your local bake sale; go ahead, contribute a cake! Or if you simply crave your favorite cookie, this is your reference guide to recreating it. Whether you're bringing, buying or just baking for the family, there's something for everyone and every occasion.

BAKE SALE BASICS

———◆———

Have you ever been in charge of a bake sale, or been asked to simply contribute a cookie? It's hard to go through life without connecting to this experience in some way. If you belong to a group that has ever benefited from the proceeds of a bake sale, consider yourself involved. The strategies in this section include helpful fund-raising ideas for many types of related activities.

If you're months or miles away from the next area bake sale (or if you have an overwhelming urge for oatmeal cookies "the way Mom made them"), you can skip this section. Satisfy your craving and head straight to the recipes!

TYPES OF BAKE SALES

Bake sales are something like flowers: There are "perennials" and "annuals." Both types perform a valuable function for the organizations they serve.

PERENNIAL BAKE SALES are a predictable routine. Monday-morning muffin breaks, Friday after-school brownie bazaars and Sunday church social cookies and coffee all fall into this category. These bake sales tend to be low-key weekly rituals. Frequently their purpose is to provide a self-perpetuating source of refreshment.

Funds raised by perennial bake sales usually replenish ingredients for the following week, and any proceeds are collected in a kitty. At the end of each year, this money might help finance a field trip, pay for the school prom decorations or help paint the church. Perennial bake sales rely solely on "built-in customers," with the club, church, school, team, office or other organization.

ANNUAL BAKE SALES are special events that commonly tie into holidays or seasonal activities. They are locally promoted to encourage a large community turnout. This type of bake sale is often held in conjunction with popular annual attractions such as school carnivals, church bazaars or flea markets. The fiscal goals of annual bake sales tend to be more ambitious than those of perennial sales; therefore THE CAUSE must be publicized along with the actual bake sale. The public always turns out to support a function that benefits a popular worthy cause…so spread the word!

A FEW EXAMPLES OF ANNUAL BAKE SALES LINKED TO HOLIDAY OR SEASONAL THEMES:

"VALENTINE CHOCOLATE SWEETHEART SALE":

February is a dreary month, and everyone is looking to break their New Year's resolution/post-holiday diets. Chocoholics take heart: This is your month to splurge! The Valentine's Day theme is perfect for a bake sale, provided that all of the products are CHOCOLATE. My high school used to hold a special chocolate bake sale in conjunction with the annual Sweetheart Dance. Stick to small treats: cupcakes, brownies, cookies and candies are good choices. Use heart motifs, doilies, red or pink cellophane, etc. for decoration and packaging.

"EASTER BUNNY BAKE OFF":

This type of sale is usually held between the week of Palm Sunday and Easter. Homemade breakfast breads and sweet rolls are very popular, as are Easter cakes and desserts. Be sure to include hand-decorated baskets filled with colorful cookies and candies, wrapped up with cellophane and bows. These are quickly grabbed up for Easter morning gifts (no matter how old the "child" is!).

Having the Easter bunny dressed in costume and waiting to greet the kids is a festive touch. So is holding a traditional "Easter Egg Roll" contest on the lawn.

"MAY DAY FLOWER FETE":

This is one time when a bake sale takes back seat to the featured event: flowers. The principle for conducting the flower sale is the same as the bake sale. Donations of flowers (and clippings from blossoming trees) are collected from your group—which always generates a lot of enthusiasm among members with a green thumb. It's an opportunity for everyone to show off their garden. During the period between May Day and Mother's Day, lilacs, jonquils, daffodils, tulips, narcissus, redbud, dogwood, cherry and apple blossoms are in bloom. Display your flowers in buckets of fresh water to create custom bouquets. Make up arrangements for customers on the spot by wrapping their selections in waxed florist paper and tying with ribbon. To add to that feel of a garden party, bake dainty cookies, tarts and teacakes to sell alongside the flowers.

FOURTH OF JULY BERRY BASH:

A "berry bash" is a combination bake sale and ice cream social, featuring the true treats of summer: strawberries, raspberries, blackberries and blueberries. Everything edible is based on berries, from blueberry muffins to raspberry bars. Serve up fresh strawberries over homemade shortcake, or bring on the ice cream freezers and scoop out rich strawberry ice cream. This event combines beautifully with barbecues, picnics and fireworks displays!

BACK-TO-SCHOOL APPLE SALE:

This is a terrific harvest theme for a September bake sale. Bring bales of hay and bushels of apples into the schoolyard to help set the scene. For this sale, concentrate on apple treats: cakes, cookies, bars and pies. (Don't forget to check out the recipe for Cheesy Apple Pizza on page 98. By the slice, it's a bestseller!) I happen to think a Back-to-School Apple Sale is a great way to break the ice on orientation day.

THE GREAT PUMPKIN FESTIVAL:

The "Great Pumpkin" is the guest of honor at this October bake sale, which incorporates home-baked harvest favorites with Halloween "goblin goodies." Pumpkin pies, cakes, cookies, bars, muffins, breads, even candied pumpkin are featured. Don't overlook other popular products that reflect the Halloween theme: caramel apples (with candy corn Jack o'lantern faces), popcorn balls (wrapped in orange cellophane), even chocolate "black cat" cupcakes. Naturally the bake sale attendants should be dressed in

Halloween costumes. "Witches' brew" (hot cocoa) can also be sold with orange marshmallow pumpkins floating on top. For a festive touch, provide decorated trick-or-treat bags for customers to haul home their bake sale goodies.

THANKSGIVING PARADE OF PIES:

Thanksgiving is one holiday where pie is a prerequisite on the dessert menu. A "Parade of Pies" is just that, a bake sale devoted exclusively to pies: mincemeat, apple crumb, pecan, sweet potato, chess, maple walnut and (of course) every version of pumpkin pie ever imagined! Decades ago, the task of baking pies was best left to those gifted few with true pastry talent. But now there's no reason for anyone to panic about pie baking; with so many excellent frozen and prepared crusts on the market, everyone can bake a pie like a pro. *Freshness* is the key to selling pies at the peak of perfection. Since most people will be bringing the pies home for their holiday dinner, it's best to plan this sale as close to Thanksgiving as possible.

CHRISTMAS BAZAAR/COOKIE & CANDY EXCHANGE:

Christmas bazaars, complete with fresh trees, ornaments and handmade decorations, are a natural setting for a "Cookie & Candy Exchange." This type of bake sale is an efficient way for busy holiday shoppers to collect a beautiful assortment of homemade delicacies. Each participating baker is assigned one recipe (often his or her specialty). The day before the sale, a "packaging committee" can arrange cookie combinations in attractive gift baskets, boxes or containers. This saves time for everyone involved. (As you probably know, it's much easier to concentrate on baking one big batch of toffee bars than a dozen different types.) What an easy way to amass a spectacular Christmas cookie selection.

ORGANIZING THE ORGANIZATION

Getting a bake sale off the ground takes organizing. It's wise to choose committee members and a chairman before delegating any duties. The chairman in charge of the bake sale needn't be a Betty Crocker…but should know who is or, more importantly, who isn't! Not that it takes a great deal of skill to master any of the most common bake sale treats. However, there are always those who either lack the patience to bake or are baffled by any food that isn't zapped in a microwave. Just remember, everyone has his own special talent. The chairman's job is to find that talent and put it to good use. Perhaps it lies in telephoning volunteers, typing flyers, writing labels, purchasing materials, packaging products or promoting or supervising the actual bake sale booth.

Perennial bake sales are approached more casually, with duties frequently rotated among members from week to week. The format and bake sale "menu" are often such a standard routine that everyone knows what to expect. Actually, the most important job for some bake sales might just be that of "phone captain" (the person who calls everyone a couple of days in advance to tell them what to bake…then calls everyone the morning of the sale and reminds them to bring it! I'm guilty of such memory lapses. As a twelve-year-old Girl Scout, I was always leaving my applesauce bars at home on the breakfast table. This made me a little unpopular with the "cookie committee").

Annual bake sales require more extensive planning. Usually the committee must decide upon a theme, or how to coordinate the bake sale with the theme of the companion event. (See "Types of Bake Sales" for ideas.) Bake sale classics are always featured, but don't fall into the clone syndrome. Nine versions of lemon bars will be about as exciting as nine versions of baked bean casseroles at a potluck supper! Try to encourage individuality and limit duplicate donations. First ask each volunteer to suggest a few of his or her specialties. Make a list and coordinate the bake sale menu accordingly. You'll want to include as many traditional items as possible and still be innovative. How about an old-fashioned cake walk contest? (It's similar to musical chairs, with a luscious layer cake for the grand prize.) This always draws a crowd over to the cake booth.

Sometime you may want large quantities of a specific product for your bake sale theme. If you're going to mass-produce homemade pumpkin pies, you might circulate the same recipe to all of the contributors. In this instance, conformity is the goal. Standard ingredients and baking pans for everyone involved will improve the quality control. Always take advantage of seasonal themes and produce to increase the public interest. Now you're ready to go put on a world class bake sale!

SPREADING THE WORD

Through the years, many great bake sales got that way by word of mouth. As their reputation grows, so does their attendance. If your bake sale is new on the block, it's important to spread the word. This will take some promoting, but remember, the best publicity is FREE!

Most perennial bake sales are "in-house" operations, where the customers are also the sponsors. (In other words, the same people selling are also buying.) An example of this would be a bake sale during a P.T.A. meeting coffee break. This type of weekly sale is self-perpetuating and requires little more than a casual announcement, or a sign in the hallway.

On the other hand, annual bake sales are a big deal and require more aggressive promotion. The objective is to draw a large crowd from your local community (which is why they are often held in conjunction with special events). Posters, flyers and banners are always effective, but don't overlook your local media for public support. Send a press release (even a photo from last year's event) to your newspaper. Food editors are often delighted to use such material, along with some unique recipes to be featured at the bake sale. "Community Billboard" announcements are aired by most radio stations as a public service. Local T.V. stations may also be interested in covering the event. These are busy places with busy people, so here's an attention-getting tip: send your press releases to local radio and T.V. stations with a "goodies gift." This could be any attractively packaged cake, pie, bread or cookie that's best suited to be your bake sale ambassador. Call the station in advance and find out to whom it should be addressed, then hand-deliver it to that department. You'll soon see that a pie is worth a thousand words, or that the way to an anchorman's heart is through his stomach!

THE BUSINESS OF BAKE SALES

As with any business, the whole point of a bake sale is to earn profits. However, these profits are being raised for a specific goal, organization or charity. Commercial bakeries, pastry shops and caterers try to net *at least* a 100% profit margin over their costs (ingredients and materials, labor and overhead). I say *at least 100%* because the free enterprise system is really based on what the market will bear.

For example, at certain times of the year, some items will be at a premium (like pumpkin pies on the day before Thanksgiving). After the item is out of season, it quickly loses demand and the price is slashed. Obviously food products are not only seasonal, they're perishable; nothing has a shorter shelf life. Which is why bakeries drastically reduce the prices of "day-old" breads and pastries.

Unfortunately, a bake sale cannot resort to the option of a day-old rack. Most of these events are one-day affairs, which works to their advantage: The customers are drawn to the fresh, homemade quality of the baked goods. But don't be left holding the bag of brownies by day's end! It's important to price products according to what *your* market will bear.

And how much is that? Luckily there are many factors in a bake sale's favor. First, your costs are considerably less than a commercial operation: Volunteer labor is free. Retail space for a bake sale is usually on the organization's own property (or public property), and there's generally no rent involved. Operating costs (such as utilities and equipment) are absorbed by the volunteers, baking out of their homes. In many bake sales, the ingredients are considered part of the volunteer's donation. The exception to this is when ingredients are unusually expensive (as with fruitcakes), or when the responsibility falls on just a few people to produce a large quantity of a particular item. On such occasions, funds from the bake sale are used to reimburse ingredient costs. The costs of packaging materials in large quantities (such as baskets, gift boxes and ribbons) are frequently shared by the group. Individual projects of a personalized nature are a different matter; here the cost may also be absorbed by each baker. (Some people prefer to give a special family recipe a unique "signature" package.)

Finally, always remember that your major advantage over a commercial operation is THE CAUSE. A bake sale has a built-in public waiting to buy the products for a common goal. Even if Mrs. Smith bakes awful brownies, the customers will probably be forgiving. But the point of this book is to help Mrs. Smith bake better brownies (or you can always make her chief in charge of brownie boxes!).

SETTING UP SHOP

After you've determined who is going to bake what and when they're going to bring it, it's time to figure out where and how you're going to set up shop. This is a fairly simple task, provided you don't have to make a lot of special arrangements. For example: If you need to rent a refrigerator or freezer, be sure you have a suitable electrical outlet and that you allow at least 12 hours for the unit to chill down. (Putting ice cream in a hot freezer is an exercise in futility—believe me, I've done it!) If your organization has refrigeration in the kitchen or dining hall, you have more flexibility. Try to keep the bake sale adjacent to it—that is, if you need it. Food spoilage is serious stuff and can make people sick. That's why most of the recipes in this book are designed to be held at room temperature. (Recently microwaves have been brought into some bake sales to heat up fresh muffins and pie by the slice.) Unless it's critical to the theme (as in an ice cream social), stay away from chilled foods.

Tables are the top priority. Most bake sale "booths" are simply tables draped with cloths. Most organizations have a lot of long tables on hand that will work perfectly. Use baskets or trays for different items, and arrange them at "stations" (pies at one table — cakes on another). Descriptions should be well displayed and prices clearly marked on a sign in front of each item. There should be at least one calculator and cash box; if it's a big bake sale, it's more efficient to have a calculator and cash box for each table. Be sure to start the sale off with plenty of small change to break larger bills. Ask the attendants to keep track of what sells first or seems to be the most popular item. This will help in planning the next bake sale.

THE
COOKIE KING

CHAMPION CHOCOLATE CHIP COOKIES

DOUBLE CHOCOLATE CHUNK COOKIES

PEANUT BUTTER CHOCOLATE KISS "KOOKIES"

WHITE CHOCOLATE CHUNK COOKIES

MIDGET MINI CHIP MERINGUES

MAMMOTH MACADAMIA CHOCOLATE CHIP COOKIES

M&M COOKIES

HEATH BAR CRUNCH COOKIES

OATMEAL CHOCOLATE CHIP COOKIES

CHOCOLATE CHIP ROCKY ROAD PIZZA

THE COOKIE KING

If a contest were held for America's favorite cookie, the all-time champ would be CHOCOLATE CHIP. No wonder it's the bestseller at every bake sale. Through the years, we've witnessed an entire family of cookies grow up (from little bitty, bite-sized baby cookies to great big, gooey, grown-up gourmet cookies). We've taken the traditional Toll House recipe (Mom made it from the back of the bag) and turned it into a chocolate chip, rocky road pizza. But by any name (morsels, bits, kisses or chunks), the cookie made with chocolate chips is a classic.

"CHIP TIPS"

There's a whole new marketplace of chocolate chips and chunks competing for your attention…calling out, "Eat me"! But before you buy, it's important to know what you're buying. Even the traditional Nestle Toll House® morsel has taken on new sizes and a new shape.

At the beginning of my career, I was recruited as a media spokesperson for Nestle. I was introducing what was then called the "Maxi-Morsel" to the test market: Bangor, Maine. After hours of "de-programming" by the company execs, I finally learned to call chocolate chips…chocolate "morsels." But all my training was in vain. As soon as I walked into the tiny T.V. studio, I realized that I'd have to learn the local language. In Maine, chocolate morsels are chocolate *"bits."* So much for semantics…a chip is a chip is chocolate!

And now there are so many choices to choose from: milk chocolate chips and chunks, and European-style; dark sweet chocolate chips and chunks, in addition to the standard semisweet chocolate chips and chunks. There are even miniature chips and minted chips.

Which introduces another category of chips: confectionery compounds. These include the popular butterscotch and peanut butter morsels often baked into cookies as is, or melted down. These contain vegetable oil instead of cocoa butter and are *not* a chocolate product. On the other hand, white "chocolate" chips contain cocoa butter but not chocolate liquor, so they can't really be called chocolate, either.

To further confuse the issue, "chocolate flavored" chips are also a confectionery compound that mimics semisweet chocolate chips at a cheaper price; they often appear as a generic store brand. These won't deliver the rich flavor you expect in a traditional cookie recipe, and results can be disappointing. But they do have one virture: they don't bloom.

"Bloom" is what has happened to any streaky-gray chocolate bar you open on a summer day. The chocolate melts, then rehardens and the cocoa butter rises to the surface—not a pretty sight. Because confectionery compounds contain vegetable oil, this doesn't occur. When dipping candies or decorating cookies calling for melted chocolate, you might consider using those "chocolate flavored" (confectionery compound) chips. It's the easiest way to achieve a glossy chocolate sheen without tempering.

Tempering is the technique used by professional chocolatiers on the finest chocolate. It eliminates bloom and produces a lovely luster. It's tricky to do at home without the pro's temperature-controlled machinery, but it can be done.

MELTING METHODS

No chocolate—unsweetened, semisweet, dark sweet, milk, white chocolate or confectionery compound—should ever be heated above 110°F (43°C). Otherwise the chocolate will scorch and stiffen. Also, always use *dry* pans and utensils. This is important because the tiniest amount of liquid will cause chocolate to stiffen or tighten up. The addition of solid shortening or oil (not butter) helps reduce bloom. But to temper chocolate the old-fashioned way:

Finely chop chocolate (or use minichips) and divide into thirds. Melt two-thirds of chocolate to 110°F (43°C), stirring until smooth. Remove from heat source and blend in the remaining one-third of chocolate. Do not let this tempered chocolate go below 90°F (32°C). (If this sounds too difficult, just use the shortening method...or "chocolate flavored" chips.)

TAKING THE HEAT

DOUBLE BOILER: A great way to control temperature, when used at least 1 inch above very hot—not boiling—water. DO NOT ALLOW ANY STEAM TO CONTACT THE CHOCOLATE.

MICROWAVE: Very easy, if a little unpredictable (no two ovens are exactly alike). Generally, 1 ounce of chocolate will melt in a minute or two. I say "melt" but it really doesn't. Look for the surface to turn very glossy; that's your cue to stir it smooth.

HOT PLATE: My favorite method! There's no steam or over-microwaving involved. I just plug my hot plate (or even my coffeecup warmer) into the wall and the chocolate takes care of itself.

Remember, cooking is supposed to be creative. Go ahead and experiment with different types of chocolate chips and chunks. But keep in mind that certain chocolates will act differently in the oven than others. For example, milk chocolate, white chocolate and all confectionery compound chips will become *harder* after baking—which is why "The Cookie King" (the classic chocolate chip version) is traditionally made with semisweet chocolate.

CHAMPION CHOCOLATE CHIP COOKIES

MAKES
8 dozen

2¼ CUPS ALL PURPOSE FLOUR

1 TEASPOON BAKING SODA

1 TEASPOON SALT

1 CUP (2 sticks) BUTTER OR MARGARINE, SOFTENED

¾ CUP GRANULATED SUGAR

¾ CUP FIRMLY PACKED LIGHT BROWN SUGAR

1 TEASPOON VANILLA EXTRACT

2 EGGS

12-OUNCE PACKAGE SEMISWEET CHOCOLATE CHIPS

1 CUP CHOPPED PECANS OR WALNUTS

PREHEAT OVEN TO 375°F (190°C).

In small bowl, combine flour, soda and salt; set aside. In large bowl, cream butter, sugars and vanilla until smooth and fluffy. Beat in eggs one at a time. Blend in flour mixture, chocolate chips and nuts. Drop by rounded teaspoonfuls onto ungreased baking sheets. Bake 8 to 10 minutes until golden. Cool 2 minutes, then gently transfer to racks with spatula.

"Some people just can't seem to get enough chocolate." Sound familiar? Then try teaming rich chocolate cookies filled with gooey chocolate chunks.

★ ★ ★

DOUBLE CHOCOLATE CHUNK COOKIES

1	CUP (2 sticks) BUTTER OR MARGARINE, SOFTENED
3/4	CUP FIRMLY PACKED DARK BROWN SUGAR
1/2	CUP GRANULATED SUGAR
1	TEASPOON VANILLA EXTRACT
1	EGG
1/4	CUP UNSWEETENED COCOA POWDER
2	CUPS ALL PURPOSE FLOUR
1	TEASPOON BAKING SODA
1/2	TEASPOON SALT
	8-OUNCE BAR SEMISWEET CHOCOLATE, COARSELY CHOPPED

MAKES 2½ to 3 dozen

PREHEAT OVEN TO 375°F (190°C).

In large bowl, cream butter and sugars until light and fluffy. Beat in vanilla. Blend in egg and cocoa, then flour, soda and salt, beating at low speed until mixture forms a stiff dough. Stir in chocolate chunks. Drop by rounded tablespoonfuls 2 inches apart on ungreased baking sheet. Bake 8 to 12 minutes until set. Cool 2 minutes, then transfer to racks with spatula.

THE COOKIE KING

This old-fashioned favorite was a fad during the '50s.

★ ★ ★

PEANUT BUTTER CHOCOLATE KISS "KOOKIES"

1¾ CUPS ALL PURPOSE FLOUR

½ CUP GRANULATED SUGAR

½ CUP FIRMLY PACKED DARK BROWN SUGAR

1 TEASPOON BAKING SODA

½ TEASPOON SALT

½ CUP BUTTER-FLAVORED SHORTENING

½ CUP CREAMY PEANUT BUTTER

2 TABLESPOONS MILK

1 TEASPOON VANILLA EXTRACT

1 EGG

GRANULATED SUGAR

4 DOZEN HERSHEY'S KISSES

PREHEAT OVEN TO 375°F (190°C).

In large bowl, combine flour, sugars, soda, salt, shortening, peanut butter, milk, vanilla and egg. Beat at low speed until mixture forms firm dough. Shape into 1-inch balls and roll in sugar. Place 2 inches apart on ungreased baking sheet. Bake 10 to 12 minutes until golden. Remove from oven and IMMEDIATELY top each cookie with a chocolate kiss, pressing firmly (cookie will crack around edges) Cool 2 minutes, then remove from cookie sheets with spatula.

Fudgy, dark chocolate cookies are flecked with big chunks of creamy white chocolate.

★ ★ ★

WHITE CHOCOLATE CHUNK COOKIES

MAKES
4 dozen

3   CUPS ALL PURPOSE FLOUR

¾   CUP UNSWEETENED COCOA POWDER

¾   TEASPOON BAKING SODA

½   TEASPOON SALT

1   CUP (2 sticks) BUTTER OR MARGARINE, SOFTENED

1   CUP GRANULATED SUGAR

1   CUP FIRMLY PACKED DARK BROWN SUGAR

2   EGGS

   8-OUNCE BAR WHITE CHOCOLATE, COARSELY CHOPPED

PREHEAT OVEN TO 350°F (175°C).

Combine flour, cocoa, soda and salt in medium mixing bowl. In large mixing bowl, cream butter and sugars until light and fluffy. Beat in eggs one at a time. Blend in flour mixture. Stir in white chocolate chunks. Drop dough by tablespoonfuls 3 inches apart on lightly greased baking sheets. Flatten slightly. Bake 8 to 10 minutes until set. Cool 1 minute. Gently transfer to racks with spatula.

*These are often called
"forgotten cookies"
because they're left in the
oven overnight.*

★ ★ ★

MIDGET MINI CHIP MERINGUES

MAKES
4 dozen

2　EGG WHITES, ROOM TEMPERATURE

$^1/_8$　TEASPOON SALT

$^1/_8$　TEASPOON CREAM OF TARTAR

$^1/_2$　TEASPOON VANILLA EXTRACT

$^3/_4$　CUP SUGAR

$1^1/_2$　CUPS SEMISWEET CHOCOLATE MINICHIPS

PREHEAT OVEN TO 250°F (120°C).

Beat egg whites, salt, cream of tartar and vanilla with electric mixer until soft peaks form. Add $^1/_2$ cup sugar in a thin, steady stream, beating constantly, until meringue stands in stiff, shiny peaks. Stir chips and remaining sugar together in another bowl. Gently fold into meringue. Drop by teaspoonfuls onto baking sheets lined with parchment paper. Bake 30 minutes. Turn off heat and leave in oven, with door closed, overnight. Store in airtight container to retain crispness.

MAMMOTH MACADAMIA CHOCOLATE CHIP COOKIES

MAKES

16 large

cookies

1	CUP (2 sticks) BUTTER OR MARGARINE
1	CUP FIRMLY PACKED LIGHT BROWN SUGAR
1½	TEASPOONS VANILLA EXTRACT
1	EGG
1¾	CUPS ALL PURPOSE FLOUR
1	TEASPOON BAKING SODA
½	TEASPOON SALT
	6-OUNCE PACKAGE WHITE CHOCOLATE CHIPS OR CHUNKS
1	CUP (3½-OUNCE JAR) MACADAMIA NUTS, COARSELY CHOPPED
½	CUP TOASTED COCONUT

PREHEAT OVEN TO 375°F (190°C).

In large bowl, cream butter with brown sugar and vanilla until light and fluffy. Beat in egg. Blend in flour, soda and salt. Stir in chocolate, nuts and coconut. Shape into 2-inch balls and place 4 inches apart on ungreased cookie sheet. Bake 15 to 20 minutes until golden. Cool 2 minutes. Transfer to racks with large spatula.

*Opposite: Great Pumpkin Cookies (left), page 84;
Candy Cane Cookies (center), page 86;
Sugar Cookies (right), page 90*

THE COOKIE KING

Extra large, kid-sized cookies.

★ ★ ★

M&M COOKIES

½ CUP (1 stick) BUTTER OR MARGARINE, SOFTENED

½ CUP BUTTER-FLAVORED SHORTENING

¾ CUP FIRMLY PACKED BROWN SUGAR

1½ TEASPOONS VANILLA EXTRACT

1 EGG

1¾ CUPS ALL PURPOSE FLOUR

1 TEASPOON BAKING SODA

½ TEASPOON SALT

1½ CUPS M&M CANDIES

MAKES
14 jumbo
cookies

In large bowl, cream butter and shortening with brown sugar and vanilla until light and fluffy. Beat in egg. Stir flour, baking soda and salt together in separate bowl. Blend into egg mixture. Fold in 1 cup M&Ms. Cover dough with plastic wrap and refrigerate for easier handling.

PREHEAT OVEN TO 350°F (175°C).

Shape dough into 2-inch balls. Place 4 inches apart on an ungreased baking sheet. Use remaining ½ cup candies to decorate tops of cookies. Bake 15 to 20 minutes until golden. Cool 2 minutes. Gently transfer to racks with large spatula.

Opposite: Cheesy Apple Pizza, page 98

These crisp toffee chip cookies are a little fragile. I suggest lining baking sheets with parchment paper, and removing the cookies only when completely cooled.

★ ★ ★

HEATH BAR CRUNCH COOKIES

MAKES
4 dozen

1½   CUPS (3 sticks) BUTTER OR MARGARINE, SOFTENED
1½   CUPS SUGAR
2   TEASPOONS VANILLA EXTRACT
3   CUPS SIFTED ALL PURPOSE FLOUR
½   TEASPOON BAKING SODA
6   HEATH BARS, CHOPPED

Cream butter, sugar and vanilla until light and fluffy. Mix flour and soda together. Blend into butter mixture with candy. Shape dough into 2 rolls, about 2 inches in diameter. Wrap in plastic and chill until firm.

PREHEAT OVEN TO 375°F (190°C).

Cut rolls into ¼-inch slices and place 4 inches apart on baking sheets lined with parchment paper (cookies will spread). Bake 15 minutes. When completely cool, gently lift from parchment with spatula.

The addition of oatmeal and cinnamon to chocolate chip cookies makes a great coffee break treat.

OATMEAL CHOCOLATE CHIP COOKIES

$2^1/_4$	CUPS ALL PURPOSE FLOUR
2	CUPS FIRMLY PACKED LIGHT BROWN SUGAR
1	TEASPOON BAKING SODA
$^1/_2$	TEASPOON SALT
1	TEASPOON CINNAMON
1	CUP (2 sticks) BUTTER OR MARGARINE, SOFTENED
2	EGGS
1	TEASPOON VANILLA EXTRACT
2	CUPS QUICK-COOKING ROLLED OATS
$^1/_2$	CUP CHOPPED WALNUTS
	6-OUNCE PACKAGE SEMISWEET CHOCOLATE CHIPS

MAKES
2½ to
3 dozen

PREHEAT OVEN TO 350°F (175°C).

In large bowl, combine flour, brown sugar, soda, salt, cinnamon, butter, eggs and vanilla. Beat at medium speed 1 to 2 minutes. Stir in oatmeal, walnuts and chocolate chips. Drop by well rounded tablespoonfuls 2 inches apart on ungreased cookie sheets. Bake 12 to 15 minutes until golden. Cool 2 minutes, then carefully transfer to racks with spatula.

This "cookie" is a kid's dream-come-true. I once concocted it at a teenage slumber party. We forgot to put the marshmallows and chocolate chips on top until the pizza had cooled, so we melted the topping with a hair dryer!

★ ★ ★

CHOCOLATE CHIP ROCKY ROAD PIZZA

2¼	CUPS ALL PURPOSE FLOUR
1	TEASPOON BAKING SODA
1	TEASPOON SALT
1	CUP (2 sticks) BUTTER OR MARGARINE, SOFTENED
2	EGGS
¾	CUP GRANULATED SUGAR
¾	CUP FIRMLY PACKED BROWN SUGAR
1	TEASPOON VANILLA EXTRACT
	12-OUNCE PACKAGE SEMISWEET CHOCOLATE CHIPS
1	CUP CHOPPED PECANS OR WALNUTS
	Topping (recipe follows)

MAKES one 14-inch pizza

PREHEAT OVEN TO 375°F (190°C).

Combine flour, soda, and salt in bowl. In another bowl, cream butter and sugars until blended. Beat in eggs and vanilla extract. Mix in dry ingredients, along with chocolate chips and nuts. Pat into 14-inch round pizza pan that has been sprayed with nonstick coating. Bake 25 minutes. Remove from oven and immediately sprinkle topping over cookie crust. Let stand about 5 minutes, then swirl with spatula. Cool completely. Cut into wedges before serving or selling. (This is usually purchased by the piece.)

Topping

6-OUNCE PACKAGE SEMISWEET CHOCOLATE CHIPS
1 CUP MINIATURE MARSHMALLOWS
1 CUP PECAN PIECES

Combine chocolate chips, marshmallows, and pecans.

"Slumber Party Style"

Bake the cookie dough ahead of time in pizza pan and allow to cool. Combine topping in a bowl and scatter over pizza. Now for the entertainment! Place the pizza in the center of a circle of teenagers. Pass around a hair dryer, and let them take turns melting the topping. For safety, don't get any closer than four inches from the topping.

BROWNIE & BAR BAZAAR

AMERICA'S BEST BROWNIE
(Basic Brownie, Chocolate Chunky, Coffee-Toffee and Spicy Black Pepper)

BANGOR BIG FAT FUDGE BROWNIES • PANDA BEAR BROWNIES

PEANUT BUTTER BROWNIES • BUTTERSCOTCH BLONDIES • BANANA BREAKFAST BARS

APPLE BUTTER BARS • TOFFEE TURTLE BARS • PRALINE PECAN BARS

BERRY CRUMB BARS • MAPLE WALNUT BARS • CHERRY CHEESECAKE BARS

HOOSIER BARS • BEE'S KNEES BARS • JAM DANDY DATE BARS

BEST-LOVED LEMON BARS
(Traditional Lemon, Mandarin Orange, Coconut Key Lime, Almond Amaretto, and Cherry Bon Bon)

PLYMOUTH PUMPKIN BARS • LAZY LAYER BARS • "ORIGINAL SIN" BARS

CLASSIC CRISPY BARS
(Toasted Rice, Tutti Frutti, Rocky Road and Scotcheroo)

BROWNIE & BAR BAZAAR

Since the chocolate chip cookie holds the prestigious title of "American Bake Sale Bestseller," we must award first runner-up to the brownie. Coming in a close third…lemon bars.

Chocolaty, chewy, crispy, crunchy—all bars share one common bond. They're *easy.* You don't have to cut them out, or roll them into dozens of perfectly uniform balls. And you don't encounter that familiar frustration of drop cookies, when seemingly well-spaced dough bakes into an indistinguishable mass. Who knows? Perhaps that's how bar cookies were invented!

"BAR NONE"

Bar none—anybody can bake these. If you don't have the time or talent to bake anything else, you *can* bake these. Brownies and bars are hard to mess up...and make very little mess. Simple, yet sophisticated bars have become the cookie of choice for beginning bakers (and pros appreciate their versatility). Even the average brownie can be transformed to a new level of elegance with the addition of crushed toffee, coffee, or would you believe, black pepper! Basic lemon bars take on a whole new character with key lime juice, rum or amaretto liqueur. There's even an upscale version of the classic rice crispie treat—chocolate, marshmallows and pecans turn this into a rocky road confection. So the next time your child comes home with a "Bake Sale Tomorrow" note pinned to his coat, don't panic. Bake some bars.

Try variations for entirely new taste sensations.

★ ★ ★

AMERICA'S BEST BROWNIE

2 dozen

¹/₂   CUP (1 stick) BUTTER OR MARGARINE

2   OUNCES UNSWEETENED CHOCOLATE

1   CUP SUGAR

1   TEASPOON VANILLA EXTRACT

2   EGGS

¹/₂   TEASPOON SALT

¹/₂   TEASPOON BAKING POWDER

²/₃   CUP ALL PURPOSE FLOUR

¹/₂   CUP CHOPPED TOASTED PECANS

      Fudge Glaze (optional; recipe follows)

PREHEAT OVEN TO 350°F (175°C).

Grease and lightly flour bottom only of an 8- or 9-inch square pan. In large saucepan, melt butter and chocolate over low heat, stirring constantly. Remove from heat and cool slightly. Blend in sugar and vanilla. Beat in eggs one at a time. Stir in salt, baking powder, flour, and pecans. Spread in pan and bake 20 to 25 minutes until set in center (do not overbake). If desired, spread brownies with chocolate glaze. Cool completely, then cut into squares.

Chocolate Glaze

1	OUNCE UNSWEETENED CHOCOLATE
3	TABLESPOONS BUTTER OR MARGARINE
1	CUP POWDERED SUGAR
1	TEASPOON VANILLA EXTRACT
1 to 3	TABLESPOONS WARM MILK

Melt chocolate and butter in small saucepan. Blend in sugar and vanilla with wire whisk. Add enough milk to make a smooth, spreadable glaze.

Variations ★ ★ ★ ★ ★ ★ ★ ★ ★ ★ ★ ★ ★ ★ ★ ★ ★

SPICY BLACK PEPPER BROWNIES: Add 1 teaspoon cinnamon and 1 teaspoon cracked black pepper to batter.

CHOCOLATE CHUNKY BROWNIES: Add ½ cup raisins and 4 ounces chopped semisweet chocolate to batter.

COFFEE-TOFFEE BROWNIES: Substitute firmly packed dark brown sugar for granulated sugar. Add 1 teaspoon instant coffee to batter. Sprinkle ½ cup crushed toffee candy over batter before baking.

I was introduced to these by the food editor of the **Bangor Daily News.** *You'll never believe her name:* **Brownie Shrumpf!** *This local legend was a charming lady in her eighties. She carried a little plastic box of her homemade toffee all around the office, offering it to visitors. (How could I refuse? During the interview I ate every last crumb.) That afternoon, I learned more about Maine than I could by reading an encyclopedia. This one's for you, Brownie… God bless!*

★ ★ ★

BANGOR BIG FAT FUDGE BROWNIES

MAKES
16

³/₄	CUP (1¹/₂ sticks) MELTED BUTTER OR MARGARINE
1¹/₂	CUPS SUGAR
2	TEASPOONS VANILLA EXTRACT
3	EGGS, SLIGHTLY BEATEN
³/₄	CUP ALL PURPOSE FLOUR
¹/₂	CUP UNSWEETENED COCOA POWDER
¹/₂	TEASPOON BAKING POWDER
¹/₂	TEASPOON SALT
	POWDERED SUGAR

PREHEAT OVEN TO 350°F (175°C).

Cream butter, sugar and vanilla in mixing bowl. Beat in eggs. In another bowl, stir together flour, cocoa, baking powder and salt with a fork. Blend dry ingredients into egg mixture; do not over-beat. Spread batter into ungreased 8-inch square pan. Bake 40 to 45 minutes until brownie begins to pull away from edges of pan. Cool completely. Dust with powdered sugar and cut into squares.

*I've also heard these
dramatic-looking
brownies referred to as
"Black & White Brownies"
and "Harlequin
Brownies."*

PANDA BEAR BROWNIES

1   CUP SUGAR

$^1/_2$ CUP VEGETABLE OIL

2   EGGS

1   TEASPOON VANILLA EXTRACT

$^2/_3$ CUP ALL PURPOSE FLOUR

$^1/_2$ CUP UNSWEETENED COCOA POWDER

$^1/_2$ TEASPOON BAKING POWDER

$^1/_2$ TEASPOON SALT

Almond Cheese Frosting (recipe follows)

Chocolate Glaze (recipe follows)

MAKES

16 to 20

PREHEAT OVEN TO 350°F (175°C).

Combine sugar, oil, eggs, vanilla, flour, cocoa, baking powder and salt in mixing bowl. Beat at low speed for 2 minutes. Spread onto greased 9-inch square pan and bake 25 minutes. Cool completely. Spread cheese frosting over bars. Chill 15 minutes. Spread warm glaze evenly over cheese frosting and chill another hour before slicing.

Almond Cheese Frosting

1   3-OUNCE PACKAGE CREAM CHEESE, SOFTENED
1   TABLESPOON BUTTER OR MARGARINE, SOFTENED
2   CUPS POWDERED SUGAR
3   TABLESPOONS MILK
½ to 1   TEASPOON ALMOND EXTRACT

Combine ingredients in mixing bowl and beat until smooth.

Chocolate Glaze

In small saucepan or microwave melt 1 ounce of semisweet chocolate with 2 tablespoons of butter or margarine. Stir until smooth.

Variations ★ ★ ★ ★ ★ ★ ★ ★ ★ ★ ★ ★ ★ ★ ★ ★ ★

ESKIMO PIE BROWNIES: Omit almond extract from filling. Substitute ½ teaspoon mint extract, ½ teaspoon vanilla extract and two drops of green food coloring.

The addition of honey-roasted peanuts to this traditional brownie recipe makes a "kid's cookie" very "grown up."

★ ★ ★

PEANUT BUTTER BROWNIES

MAKES
3 dozen

2¼	CUPS ALL PURPOSE FLOUR
2½	TEASPOONS BAKING POWDER
½	TEASPOON SALT
⅔	CUP BUTTER OR MARGARINE, SOFTENED
⅔	CUP CREAMY PEANUT BUTTER
1¼	CUPS GRANULATED SUGAR
1¼	CUPS FIRMLY PACKED DARK BROWN SUGAR
1	TEASPOON VANILLA EXTRACT
3	EGGS
1	CUP COARSELY CHOPPED HONEY-ROASTED PEANUTS
	powdered sugar

PREHEAT OVEN TO 350°F (175°C).

In small bowl, combine flour, baking powder and salt. In large bowl, cream butter, peanut butter, sugars and vanilla until smooth. Beat in eggs one at a time. Blend in flour mixture. Spread evenly in ungreased 15 x 10-inch jelly roll pan. Sprinkle surface with peanuts. Bake 35 minutes, then cool completely. Dust with powdered sugar. Cut into 2-inch squares.

BROWNIE & BAR BAZAAR

*The brownie version of
Toll House cookies.*

★ ★ ★

BUTTERSCOTCH BLONDIES

2¼   CUPS ALL PURPOSE FLOUR

2½   TEASPOONS BAKING POWDER

½   TEASPOON SALT

¾   CUP (1½ sticks) BUTTER OR MARGARINE,
     SOFTENED

½   CUP GRANULATED SUGAR

2   CUPS FIRMLY PACKED DARK BROWN SUGAR

1   TEASPOON VANILLA EXTRACT

3   EGGS
     12-OUNCE PACKAGE SEMISWEET CHOCOLATE MINICHIPS

MAKES
3 dozen

PREHEAT OVEN TO 350°F (175°C).

In small bowl, combine flour, baking powder and salt. In large bowl,
cream butter, sugars and vanilla until smooth. Beat in eggs one at a
time. Blend in flour mixture. Stir in chocolate chips. Spread evenly
in greased 10 x 15-inch jelly roll pan. Bake 35 to 40 minutes; cool.
Cut into 2-inch squares.

These are a wonderful way to start the morning in place of a muffin, to serve in a breadbasket at brunch or to send the kids off to school on the run.

★ ★ ★

BANANA BREAKFAST BARS

MAKES
4 dozen

$^3/_4$ CUP FIRMLY PACKED LIGHT BROWN SUGAR

$^1/_2$ CUP (1 stick) BUTTER OR MARGARINE, SOFTENED

12-OUNCE JAR ORANGE MARMALADE (reserve 2 tablespoons for glaze)

2 EGGS

1 TEASPOON VANILLA EXTRACT

2 CUPS ALL PURPOSE FLOUR

1 TEASPOON BAKING POWDER

$^1/_2$ TEASPOON BAKING SODA

$^1/_4$ TEASPOON SALT

2 MEDIUM-SIZE RIPE BANANAS, MASHED

$^1/_2$ CUP CHOPPED PECANS

Orange Glaze (recipe follows)

PREHEAT OVEN TO 350°F (175°C).

Cream sugar and butter together until smooth. Add marmalade, eggs, vanilla, flour, baking powder, soda, salt, mashed bananas and pecans and stir with spoon until dry ingredients are moistened. Spread batter into greased and floured 10 x 15-inch jelly roll pan. Bake 30 minutes until golden brown. Spread with glaze while warm. Cool completely before cutting into bars.

Orange Glaze

1½   CUPS POWDERED SUGAR
2   TABLESPOONS ORANGE MARMALADE
1   TABLESPOON ORANGE JUICE

Mix powdered sugar, marmalade and orange juice in small bowl until smooth.

Note: These make a great "brown bag breakfast" idea. Pack them up the night before for eating on the run. Add a box of juice and you've made breakfast on the school bus or in the car commuting to the office.

A fall favorite at New England bake sales.

★ ★ ★

APPLE BUTTER BARS

4 dozen

2	CUPS ALL PURPOSE FLOUR
1½	CUPS SUGAR
1	CUP VEGETABLE OIL
2	CUPS APPLE BUTTER
4	EGGS
2	TEASPOONS BAKING POWDER
1	TEASPOON BAKING SODA
1	TEASPOON CINNAMON
1	TEASPOON NUTMEG
½	TEASPOON CLOVES
½	TEASPOON SALT
	Lemon Cheese Frosting (recipe follows)

PREHEAT OVEN TO 350°F (175°C).

Measure all ingredients except frosting into large mixing bowl and beat at low speed until moistened, then at medium speed for 2 minutes. Pour into greased 10 x 15-inch jelly roll pan. Bake 25 to 30 minutes until toothpick inserted in center comes out clean. Cool completely. Spread with frosting and cut into 48 bars.

Lemon Cheese Frosting

2 CUPS POWDERED SUGAR

$^1/_3$ CUP BUTTER OR MARGARINE, SOFTENED

3-OUNCE PACKAGE CREAM CHEESE, SOFTENED

1 TABLESPOON LEMON JUICE

1 TEASPOON GRATED LEMON PEEL

1 TEASPOON VANILLA EXTRACT

In small bowl combine all ingredients and beat until smooth.

Variation ★ ★ ★ ★ ★ ★ ★ ★ ★ ★ ★ ★ ★ ★ ★ ★ ★

CINNAMON APPLE FROSTING: Omit lemon juice and peel from frosting. Substitute 1 tablespoon apple butter and $^1/_2$ teaspoon cinnamon.

*Rich chocolate, caramel,
and crisp pecans will
remind you of
"turtle" candy.*

★ ★ ★

TOFFEE TURTLE BARS

MAKES
3 dozen

$\frac{1}{2}$ CUP (1 stick) BUTTER OR MARGARINE, SOFTENED

1   CUP FIRMLY PACKED LIGHT BROWN SUGAR

2   CUPS ALL PURPOSE FLOUR

1   CUP BROKEN PECAN HALVES

$\frac{2}{3}$ CUP BUTTER OR MARGARINE, SOFTENED

$\frac{1}{2}$ CUP FIRMLY PACKED LIGHT BROWN SUGAR

6-OUNCE PACKAGE MILK CHOCOLATE CHIPS

PREHEAT OVEN TO 350°F (175°C).

Mix $\frac{1}{2}$ cup butter, 1 cup brown sugar and the flour until the texture of fine crumbs. Press mixture firmly into ungreased 9 x 13-inch pan. Sprinkle pecans over top and set aside. Meanwhile, combine $\frac{2}{3}$ cup butter and $\frac{1}{2}$ cup brown sugar in small, heavy saucepan. Cook, stirring, until mixture comes to a boil; boil and stir 1 minute. Pour over pecans. Bake 18 to 20 minutes until set. Remove from oven. Sprinkle with chocolate chips. Cool in pan and cut into bars.

BROWNIE & BAR BAZAAR

These elegant bars are popular throughout the southeastern United States. They are almost like a confection.

★ ★ ★

PRALINE PECAN BARS

1 PACKAGE (18½ OUNCE) YELLOW CAKE MIX
¼ CUP (½ stick) BUTTER OR MARGARINE
4 CUPS PECAN HALVES
1 CUP (2 sticks) BUTTER OR MARGARINE
1 CUP FIRMLY PACKED LIGHT BROWN SUGAR
½ CUP GRANULATED SUGAR
½ CUP HONEY
¼ CUP WHIPPING CREAM

MAKES
4 dozen

PREHEAT OVEN TO 350°F (175°C).

Blend cake mix and ¼ cup butter until crumbly. Press into bottom of ungreased 10 x 15-inch jelly roll pan. Sprinkle with pecan halves and bake 10 minutes. Meanwhile, combine 1 cup butter, sugars and honey in saucepan and bring to full boil. Boil 3 minutes. Remove from heat and blend in cream. Pour over crust and return to oven. Bake 17 to 22 minutes, until entire surface is bubbly (do not burn). Cool completely. Cut into bars.

This version is made with raspberry preserves, but don't hesitate to try strawberry, blueberry or boysenberry.

★ ★ ★

BERRY CRUMB BARS

MAKES
2 dozen

1   CUP ALL PURPOSE FLOUR

1   CUP QUICK-COOKING ROLLED OATS

½   CUP FIRMLY PACKED LIGHT BROWN SUGAR

½   TEASPOON CINNAMON

½   CUP (1 stick) BUTTER OR MARGARINE, CUT INTO CUBES

    12-OUNCE JAR RASPBERRY PRESERVES

PREHEAT OVEN TO 350°F (175°C).

Combine flour, oats, sugar and cinnamon in bowl. Cut in butter until crumbly. Pat half of crumbs into bottom of greased 9-inch square pan. Bake 10 minutes. Remove from oven and cool 10 minutes. Spread preserves over crust. Sprinkle remaining crumbs over jam and return to oven. Bake 20 to 25 minutes longer. Cool completely before cutting into bars.

MAPLE WALNUT BARS

18½-OUNCE PACKAGE YELLOW CAKE MIX
(reserve ⅔ cup)

MAKES
3 dozen

½ CUP (1 stick) MELTED BUTTER OR MARGARINE

1 EGG

½ CUP FIRMLY PACKED DARK BROWN SUGAR

1½ CUPS MAPLE SYRUP

3 EGGS

½ TEASPOON MAPLE FLAVORING OR VANILLA EXTRACT

1 CUP CHOPPED WALNUTS

PREHEAT OVEN TO 350°F (175°C).

In large mixing bowl, combine cake mix, butter and egg; mix until crumbly. Press into greased 9 x 13-inch pan. Bake 15 to 20 minutes until light golden brown. Meanwhile, combine reserved cake mix, brown sugar, syrup, eggs, and flavoring and beat until smooth. Pour over crust. Sprinkle with walnuts. Bake 30 to 35 minutes until filling is set. Cool and cut into bars.

If you prefer plain
cheesecake bars, omit
cherry preserves.
Raspberry or pineapple
preserves may also be
substituted.

★ ★ ★

CHERRY CHEESECAKE BARS

16 to 20

6   TABLESPOONS (¾ stick) BUTTER OR
    MARGARINE, SOFTENED
⅓   CUP FIRMLY PACKED LIGHT BROWN SUGAR
1   CUP ALL PURPOSE FLOUR
½   CUP BLANCHED ALMONDS, TOASTED AND CHOPPED
1   CUP CHERRY PRESERVES
    Cheesecake Filling (recipe follows)

PREHEAT OVEN TO 350°F (175°C).

Cream butter with brown sugar until well blended. Blend in flour
and almonds until mixture is crumbly. Reserve 1 cup loosely
packed crumbs for topping. Press remaining mixture into bottom
of ungreased 8-inch square pan. Bake 12 to 15 minutes until crust is
golden. Remove from oven and cool slightly while preparing filling.
Spread cherry preserves over crust and cover with cheese filling.
Sprinkle reserved crumbs evenly over filling. Bake 25 minutes
longer. Cool and cut into bars. (If not using within 24 hours, store in
refrigerator.)

Cheesecake Filling

6   TABLESPOONS SUGAR

    8-OUNCE PACKAGE CREAM CHEESE, SOFTENED

1   EGG

2   TABLESPOONS MILK

1   TABLESPOON LEMON JUICE

½   TEASPOON VANILLA OR ALMOND EXTRACT

Beat sugar and cheese together until light and fluffy. Blend in egg, milk, lemon juice and flavoring and beat until smooth.

Note: Try other types of preserves for variations—strawberry, raspberry, blueberry, or pineapple.

Honey-roasted peanuts update this Indiana classic.

★ ★ ★

HOOSIER BARS

MAKES
3 dozen

1/2	CUP GRANULATED SUGAR
1/2	CUP FIRMLY PACKED LIGHT BROWN SUGAR
1/2	CUP (1 stick) BUTTER OR MARGARINE, SOFTENED
1	TEASPOON VANILLA EXTRACT
2	EGG YOLKS
1 1/2	CUPS ALL PURPOSE FLOUR
1	TEASPOON BAKING SODA
1/2	TEASPOON SALT
	6-OUNCE PACKAGE SEMISWEET CHOCOLATE CHIPS
3/4	CUP CHOPPED HONEY-ROASTED PEANUTS
	Golden Meringue (recipe follows)

PREHEAT OVEN TO 325°F (160°C).

In large bowl, cream sugars and butter until light and fluffy. Blend in vanilla and egg yolks. Mix in flour, baking soda and salt. Press dough into bottom of greased 9 x 13-inch pan. Sprinkle chocolate chips and 1/2 cup peanuts over dough and pat in gently. Prepare meringue and spread evenly over base. Sprinkle with remaining 1/4 cup peanuts. Bake 40 to 45 minutes until golden brown. Cut into bars while warm.

Golden Meringue

2   EGG WHITES
1   CUP FIRMLY PACKED LIGHT BROWN SUGAR

Beat egg whites with electric mixer until soft peaks form. Gradually add sugar, beating until stiff peaks form.

Note: Be sure to score these bars while warm. The meringue topping tends to crackle when sliced cool.

This old Virginia recipe "originally" came from Scotland...and somewhere along the way butterscotch chips got in there. I guess that's what's called culinary evolution!

★ ★ ★

BEE'S KNEES BARS

MAKES
3 dozen

1	CUP (2 sticks) BUTTER OR MARGARINE, SOFTENED
1/3	CUP HONEY
1	TEASPOON VANILLA OR ALMOND EXTRACT
1 1/2	CUPS ALL PURPOSE FLOUR
1 1/2	CUPS QUICK-COOKING ROLLED OATS
1/2	TEASPOON SALT
	6-OUNCE PACKAGE BUTTERSCOTCH CHIPS
1/2	CUP BLANCHED SLIVERED ALMONDS
2	TABLESPOONS HONEY

PREHEAT OVEN TO 350°F (175°C).

Beat butter, 1/3 cup honey and flavoring until smooth. Blend in flour, oats and salt. Stir in butterscotch chips. Press dough into ungreased 9 x 13-inch pan. Sprinkle almonds over top and pat into dough. Brush with 2 tablespoons honey. Bake 20 to 25 minutes until golden brown. Cool completely before cutting into bars.

Make an extra batch of date jam before baking these. It's wonderful on a slice of warm cinnamon toast!

★ ★ ★

JAM DANDY DATE BARS

1½   CUPS ALL PURPOSE FLOUR

1   CUP ROLLED OATS

1   CUP FIRMLY PACKED LIGHT BROWN SUGAR

½   CUP CHOPPED WALNUTS OR PECANS

¼   TEASPOON SALT

¾   CUP (1½ sticks) BUTTER OR MARGARINE

Date Jam (recipe follows)

MAKES
3 dozen

PREHEAT OVEN TO 350°F (175°C).

Combine flour, oats, sugar, nuts and salt in large mixing bowl. Cut in butter until mixture resembles coarse meal. Reserve 2 cups for topping and press remainder into bottom of greased 9 x 13-inch pan. Spread with cooled date jam and sprinkle with reserved crumb mixture. Bake 25 to 33 minutes until golden. Cool completely, then cut into bars.

Date Jam

1½ CUPS (8-OUNCE PACKAGE) CHOPPED PITTED DATES

¼ CUP FIRMLY PACKED LIGHT BROWN SUGAR

½ CUP WATER

1 TEASPOON VANILLA EXTRACT

1 TABLESPOON BRANDY (optional)

Combine dates, sugar, water, vanilla and brandy in medium sauce-pan and bring to a boil. Simmer 5 minutes until mixture resembles a thick paste. Cool.

Note: Try doubling this date jam recipe for special gifts. Pack jam into sterilized jars. Decorate tops of jars with squares of gingham, tied with twine.

Opposite: Panda Bear Brownie (left), page 38;
America's Best Brownie (center), page 35; Peanut Butter Brownie (right), page 40
Overleaf: Orange Bars (left), page 58;
Coconut Key Lime Bars (center), page 58; Best Loved Lemon Bars (right), page 57

Next to brownies, lemon bars are probably the most popular bake sale item. For interesting variations on a classic, try Orange Bars or Coconut Key Lime Bars.

★ ★ ★

BEST LOVED LEMON BARS

1   CUP (2 sticks) BUTTER OR MARGARINE, SOFTENED

3 dozen

¼   TEASPOON SALT

½   CUP POWDERED SUGAR

2   CUPS ALL PURPOSE FLOUR

4   EGGS, SLIGHTLY BEATEN

1   TABLESPOON GRATED LEMON PEEL

5   TABLESPOONS LEMON JUICE

2   CUPS GRANULATED SUGAR

¼   CUP ALL PURPOSE FLOUR
    POWDERED SUGAR

PREHEAT OVEN TO 350°F (175°C).

Blend butter, salt, ½ cup powdered sugar and 2 cups flour to make soft dough. Press evenly into ungreased 9 x 13-inch pan. Bake 15 to 20 minutes until golden. Meanwhile, combine eggs, lemon peel, lemon juice, sugar and ¼ cup flour and blend until smooth. Pour over baked crust. Reduce heat to 325° (160°C) and bake 25 minutes until firm. Cool. Dust with powdered sugar and slice into bars.

Opposite: Chocolate Truffettes, page 82
Overleaf: Classic Crispy Bars, page 63; Marshmallow Krispie Treats, page 63;
Tutti Frutti Treats, page 63; Rocky Road Treats, page 63; Scotcheroos, page 64

Variations ★ ★ ★ ★ ★ ★ ★ ★ ★ ★ ★ ★ ★ ★ ★ ★

ORANGE BARS: Substitute orange juice and peel for lemon juice and peel. Omit powdered sugar topping. Melt 2 ounces semisweet chocolate with ¼ cup (½ stick) butter. Spread over bars as a glaze.

COCONUT KEY LIME BARS: Substitute lime juice and peel for lemon juice and peel. (If desired, add 2 drops green food coloring.) After pouring filling over crust, sprinkle with 1 cup shredded coconut.

ALMOND AMARETTO BARS: Substitute Amaretto liqueur for lemon juice. Omit lemon peel. After pouring filling over crust, sprinkle with 1 cup sliced almonds.

CHERRY BON BON BARS: Substitute maraschino cherry juice for lemon juice. Omit peel. Chop about 2 dozen well-drained cherries and add to filling. Omit powdered sugar topping. Melt 1 ounce semisweet chocolate and 1 ounce unsweetened chocolate with ¼ cup (½ stick) butter. Spread over bars as a glaze.

Cape Cod cranberries make this recipe a New England treasure, perfect for a "Pilgrim-style" Thanksgiving.

★ ★ ★

PLYMOUTH PUMPKIN BARS

MAKES
45 bars

2   CUPS ALL PURPOSE FLOUR

2   CUPS FIRMLY PACKED LIGHT BROWN SUGAR

2   TEASPOONS BAKING POWDER

2   TEASPOONS BAKING SODA

2   TEASPOONS PUMPKIN PIE SPICE

½   TEASPOON SALT

1   CUP VEGETABLE OIL

2   CUPS (16 ounces) CANNED PUMPKIN

4   EGGS

½   CUP CHOPPED WALNUTS

⅔   CUP CHOPPPED FRESH CRANBERRIES

Cranberry Glaze (recipe follows)

PREHEAT OVEN TO 350°F (175°C).

In large mixing bowl, combine flour, sugar, baking powder, baking soda, spice, salt, oil, pumpkin and eggs. Blend to moisten, then beat at medium speed for 2 minutes. Stir in walnuts and cranberries. Pour into greased 10 x 15-inch jelly roll pan. Bake 30 to 35 minutes until toothpick inserted in center comes out clean. Cool completely. Spread with cranberry glaze and cut into bars.

Cranberry Glaze

2	CUPS POWDERED SUGAR
1	TABLESPOON MELTED BUTTER
3 to 4	TABLESPOONS CRANBERRY JUICE

Blend all ingredients in small mixing bowl until smooth.

Note: These make a lovely breakfast/brunch treat on Thanksgiving morning. Everyone's too busy getting the turkey in the oven to scramble eggs or toast an English muffin. I like to pile these bars in country baskets and set them out on the kitchen table — a great way to feed morning "grazers."

Also known as Seven-Layer Bars, these are so simple that no mixing bowl is required.

★ ★ ★

LAZY LAYER BARS

MAKES

12 to 16

½ CUP (1 stick) BUTTER OR MARGARINE

1 CUP GRAHAM CRACKER CRUMBS

   6-OUNCE PACKAGE SEMISWEET
   CHOCOLATE CHIPS

   6-OUNCE PACKAGE BUTTERSCOTCH CHIPS

1 CUP FLAKED COCONUT

1 CAN (14 ounce) SWEETENED CONDENSED MILK

½ CUP CHOPPED PECANS

PREHEAT OVEN TO 350°F (175°C).

Melt butter in 9 x 13-inch pan. Sprinkle graham cracker crumbs evenly over butter. Layer next three ingredients over crumbs. Drizzle condensed milk evenly over top. Sprinkle with pecans. Bake 30 minutes. Cool completely, then cut into bars.

These are so incredibly rich that they're guaranteed to make you feel guilty.

★ ★ ★

"ORIGINAL SIN" BARS

MAKES
4 dozen

1   CUP (2 sticks) BUTTER OR MARGARINE
2   CUPS CHUNKY PEANUT BUTTER
2   CUPS GRAHAM CRACKER CRUMBS
4   CUPS (1 pound) POWDERED SUGAR
    Chocolate Glaze (recipe follows)

Melt butter with peanut butter in saucepan or microwave, stirring until smooth. Blend in graham cracker crumbs and powdered sugar until thoroughly combined. Pat into ungreased 9 x 13-inch pan. Spread with glaze. Chill before slicing.

Chocolate Glaze

    12-OUNCE PACKAGE SEMISWEET CHOCOLATE CHIPS
$^{1}/_{2}$ CUP (1 stick) BUTTER OR MARGARINE

Melt chocolate chips with butter in saucepan or microwave, blending until smooth.

CLASSIC CRISPY BARS

At first I debated whether or not it was even necessary to include "Marshmallow Krispie Treats" in the book. This obligatory bake sale bar is so universal that I sometimes wonder if the recipe is just genetically passed on to each new generation. Or perhaps it really isn't inborn. Maybe it comes from years of environmental influence—like the back of the cereal box facing you on the breakfast table every morning of your life! Well, for those people who either grew up in a cave or are growing up on oat bran, this is how it's done.

MARSHMALLOW KRISPIE TREATS

Melt ¼ cup (½ stick) butter or margarine and 5 cups miniature marshmallows in top of double boiler (or in microwave). Stir until smooth. Mix in 5 cups toasted rice cereal. With buttered fingers, press into greased 9 x 13-inch pan. Cool and cut into 24 to 30 squares.

TUTTI FRUTTI TREATS

Substitute 5 cups fruit-flavored rice cereal in recipe.

ROCKY ROAD TREATS

Melt 2 cups (12-ounce package) semisweet chocolate chips with 3 tablespoons butter or margarine in top of double boiler or in microwave. Stir in 3 cups of Cocoa Krispies and 1 cup chopped pecans. Fold in 2 cups miniature marshmallows. Press into foil-lined 9 x 13-inch pan. Chill 1 hour. Remove from pan and cut into 24 to 30 squares.

SCOTCHEROOS

Melt ½ cup peanut butter and 1 cup (6-ounce package) of butterscotch chips in top of double boiler or microwave. Stir until smooth. Mix in 5 cups toasted rice cereal. Press into foil-lined 9 x 13-inch pan. Chill 1 hour. Remove from pan and cut into 24 to 30 squares.

HOMESTYLE SWEETS & HOLIDAY TREATS

AFTER-SCHOOL APPLESAUCE COOKIES • ORIGINAL OATMEAL RAISIN COOKIES

COCONUT CORNFLAKE MACAROONS • OATMEAL SCOTCHIES • LEMON SUGAR SNAPS

SHORTNIN' BREAD • SNICKERDOODLES • HERMITS
(Homey Hermits, Holiday Hermits, Hawaiian Hermits)

GINGER JOE FROGGERS • HONEY-ROASTED PEANUT BUTTER COOKIES

IDAHO POTATO TREATS • CHOCOLATE TRUFFETTES • PHILADELPHIA "PHUDGE"

GREAT PUMPKIN COOKIES • CANDY CANE COOKIES • NUTCRACKER NUGGETS

THUMBPRINTS • SUGARPLUM SPRITZ • SUGAR COOKIE CLASSICS
(Sand Tarts, Christmas Cutouts, Sweet Hearts)

HOME STYLE SWEETS & HOLIDAY TREATS

Whether you're stuffing a lunchbox in September or a stocking in December, everyone loves cookie jar classics. Applesauce oatmeal cookies, pineapple carrot cookies and "honey" hermits make wholesome snacks for growing kids (and grownup kids!). When it comes to the holidays, no one has time to bake enough cookies. Variety is the theme. A beautiful assortment of colorful cookies and candies is as breathtaking as the first snowfall—the more the merrier! But as we all know, it's easier to bake a big batch of *one* type of cookie. (I've seen people almost lose their minds trying to bake a dozen different kinds.) That's the beauty of a bake sale and the convenience of a cookie exchange; it's an excellent opportunity to set up a cookie "swap-shop." Just bake and bring your best and come back with an incredible collection.

"SMART COOKIE"

There's a cookie to suit your style, whether you want your cookies fast and easy or flavored with the labor of love. If you shy away from baking for fear you'll fill the kitchen with flour, you're not alone. (I hate cleaning up after a rolling pin cookie project...which is why I bake drop cookies!). But there are those who find cut-out cookies very gratifying. Molded cookies are great fun to bake with your kids. So you see there's no excuse not to bake cookies.

Perhaps the biggest cookie baking problem is burned bottoms. This happens when the cookies are baked on thin, highly reflective baking sheets or if you use too low an oven rack. The solutions? Try slipping an extra baking sheet under cookies (called "double panning"). Always bake cookies in the center or sometimes even the upper oven rack. Finally, cookies bake quickly, so watch them like a hawk! Just a minute or two in baking time makes a big difference in taste and texture.

The other big baking problem is cookies that break because they stick to the pan. Always grease baking sheets when the recipe calls for it. Alternatively, a good compromise for all kinds of cookies is baking parchment. If you line your sheets with this professional baking paper, your worries are over. It not only works for any type of cookie; it practically takes care of your entire cleanup.

A fall bake sale favorite.
The rich glaze on these
cookies will remind you of
caramel apples on a stick.

AFTER-SCHOOL APPLESAUCE COOKIES

4 dozen

$1/2$	CUP BUTTER
1	CUP FIRMLY PACKED LIGHT BROWN SUGAR
1	EGG
1	CUP CHUNKY APPLESAUCE
1	TEASPOON VANILLA EXTRACT
2	CUPS ALL PURPOSE FLOUR
1	TEASPOON BAKING POWDER
1	TEASPOON EACH CINNAMON, NUTMEG AND CLOVES
$1/4$	TEASPOON SALT
1	CUP GOLDEN RAISINS
$1/2$	CUP CHOPPED WALNUTS
	Caramel Butter Glaze (recipe follows)

PREHEAT OVEN TO 350°F (175°C).

Cream butter and sugar until light and fluffy. Beat in egg, applesauce and vanilla. Mix in dry ingredients, raisins and walnuts. Drop by heaping teaspoonfuls 1 inch apart on greased baking sheets. Bake 10 minutes until lightly browned around edges. Drizzle glaze over warm cookies with spoon, then transfer cookies to cooling rack.

Caramel Butter Glaze

¹/₃   CUP BUTTER

1¹/₂   CUPS POWDERED SUGAR

¹/₄   CUP COLD WATER

1   TEASPOON VANILLA EXTRACT

Melt butter in small saucepan, stirring until it is a golden, nutty brown; do not burn. Remove from heat. Add powdered sugar, water and vanilla and whisk until smooth.

Variations ★ ★ ★ ★ ★ ★ ★ ★ ★ ★ ★ ★ ★ ★ ★ ★

PACKAGING IDEA: These are very "appeeling" when sold in "apple bags." Cut apples in half and allow to dry out overnight. Press cut sides into a red-inked stamp pad and apply apples to brown lunch bags. Fill bags with cookies and tie tops with red string or yarn.

America's favorite
oatmeal cookie.
★ ★ ★

ORIGINAL OATMEAL RAISIN COOKIES

MAKES
3½ dozen

½	CUP (1 stick) BUTTER OR MARGARINE, SOFTENED
¾	CUP GRANULATED SUGAR
¼	CUP FIRMLY PACKED DARK BROWN SUGAR
1	EGG
1	TEASPOON VANILLA EXTRACT
¾	CUP ALL PURPOSE FLOUR
½	TEASPOON BAKING SODA
½	TEASPOON CINNAMON
¼	TEASPOON SALT
1½	CUPS QUICK-COOKING ROLLED OATS
½	CUP RAISINS
½	CUP CHOPPED WALNUTS

PREHEAT OVEN TO 375°F (190°C).

Cream butter and sugars until light and fluffy. Beat in egg and vanilla. Blend in remaining ingredients to make a soft dough. Drop by rounded teaspoonfuls onto greased cookie sheets. Bake 7 to 10 minutes until edges are golden brown. Cool 1 minute, then transfer cookies to cooling rack.

These gems originated on the back of an "ancient" cereal box.

★ ★ ★

COCONUT CORNFLAKE MACAROONS

MAKES
2 dozen

1	EGG WHITE
½	CUP SUGAR
½	TEASPOON EACH VANILLA AND ALMOND EXTRACTS
⅛	TEASPOON SALT
1	CUP LIGHTLY TOASTED COCONUT
1	CUP CORNFLAKES

PREHEAT OVEN TO 350°F (175°C).

Beat egg white until stiff. Stir in sugar, flavorings, salt, coconut and cornflakes with spatula. Drop by teaspoonfuls 2 inches apart on baking sheets lined with parchment paper. Bake about 12 minutes until lightly browned. Cool on paper. Remove with spatula and store in airtight containers.

OATMEAL SCOTCHIES

2	CUPS ALL PURPOSE FLOUR
2	TEASPOONS BAKING POWDER
1	TEASPOON BAKING SODA
1	TEASPOON SALT
1	CUP (2 sticks) BUTTER OR MARGARINE, SOFTENED
1½	CUPS FIRMLY PACKED BROWN SUGAR
2	EGGS
1	TABLESPOON MILK
1½	CUPS QUICK-COOKING ROLLED OATS
	12-OUNCE PACKAGE BUTTERSCOTCH MORSELS

MAKES
4 dozen

PREHEAT OVEN TO 375°F (190°C).

In medium bowl combine flour, baking powder, soda and salt. Cream butter and brown sugar. Beat in eggs, milk and oats. Stir in dry ingredients and butterscotch morsels. Drop by tablespoonfuls 2 inches apart on greased cookie sheets. Bake 10 to 12 minutes until golden brown. Cool 5 minutes. Gently lift with spatula and cool completely on racks.

I couldn't wait for Sunday school to end so I could rush out to the church bazaar bake sale. I always headed straight to the table laden with crisp lemon cookies; if I didn't hurry, they were always sold out.

★ ★ ★

LEMON SUGAR SNAPS

1³⁄₄	CUPS ALL PURPOSE FLOUR
1	SCANT TEASPOON BAKING SODA
1	SCANT TEASPOON CREAM OF TARTAR
¹⁄₂	TEASPOON SALT
1	CUP (2 sticks) BUTTER OR MARGARINE, SOFTENED
1	CUP SUPERFINE SUGAR
1	EGG, BEATEN
	FINELY GRATED RIND OF 2 LEMONS
1	TEASPOON LEMON EXTRACT
1	TABLESPOON FRESH LEMON JUICE
	GRANULATED SUGAR

MAKES
3¹⁄₂ dozen

Mix dry ingredients in small bowl. In large bowl, cream butter and superfine sugar until light and fluffy. Beat in egg, lemon rind, extract and juice. Mix in dry ingredients. Wrap in plastic and chill dough overnight.

PREHEAT OVEN TO 325°F (160°C).

Form dough into ³⁄₄-inch balls. Place 3 inches apart on lightly greased baking sheets. Flatten balls with bottom of glass dipped in sugar. Bake 7 to 9 minutes until cookies are lightly browned around edges. Let cool 5 minutes, then lift with spatula.

*This makes an elegant gift
when baked to fit exactly
into a shallow 8-inch tin.*

★ ★ ★

SHORTNIN' BREAD

1 dozen

$^1/_2$ CUP (1 stick) BUTTER, SOFTENED

$^1/_4$ CUP FIRMLY PACKED DARK BROWN SUGAR

1 CUP ALL PURPOSE FLOUR

2 TABLESPOONS CORNSTARCH

2 TEASPOONS VANILLA EXTRACT

$^1/_2$ CUP CHOPPED TOASTED PECANS

12 PECAN HALVES

PREHEAT OVEN TO 325°F (160°C).

Cream butter and sugar. Mix in flour, cornstarch, vanilla and chopped pecans. Shape dough into 8-inch circle on ungreased baking sheet. Score into 12 wedges with knife. Decorate each wedge with pecan half. Bake for 25 to 30 minutes until shortbread looks dry but is not brown. When cool, recut shortbread along scored lines.

These were probably the very first cookies I ever baked...with a recipe from my Brownie Scout handbook. (I got my cooking badge!)

★ ★ ★

SNICKERDOODLES

½ CUP (1 stick) BUTTER OR MARGARINE, SOFTENED

1 CUP SUGAR (reserve ¼ cup)

1 EGG

1 EGG YOLK

1 TEASPOON VANILLA EXTRACT

1⅔ CUPS ALL PURPOSE FLOUR

½ TEASPOON BAKING SODA

½ TEASPOON SALT

½ TEASPOON NUTMEG

1 CUP CHOPPED WALNUTS

1 TABLESPOON CINNAMON

MAKES
2½ dozen

PREHEAT OVEN TO 375°F (190°C).

In large bowl, cream butter and ¾ cup sugar until fluffy. Beat in egg, yolk and vanilla. Mix flour, soda, salt and nutmeg in small bowl. Blend into butter mixture. Stir in walnuts. Mix reserved ¼ cup sugar and cinnamon. Shape dough into 1-inch balls and roll in cinnamon sugar. Place 2 inches apart on greased baking sheet. Bake 10 to 12 minutes. Cool 2 minutes, then lift from baking sheets with spatula and cool on racks.

HOME STYLE SWEETS & HOLIDAY TREATS

(Homey Hermits, Holiday Hermits, Hawaiian Hermits)

Like a good fruitcake, these spicy New England cookies actually improve with a little age. They remain fresh and flavorful when stored in an airtight container. Ideal for holiday cookie tins.

★ ★ ★

HERMITS

MAKES
3 dozen

¼ CUP (½ stick) BUTTER OR MARGARINE, SOFTENED

¼ CUP SHORTENING

1 CUP FIRMLY PACKED DARK BROWN SUGAR

¼ CUP FROZEN APPLE JUICE CONCENTRATE, THAWED

1 EGG

½ TEASPOON CINNAMON

½ TEASPOON NUTMEG

1¾ CUPS ALL PURPOSE FLOUR

½ TEASPOON BAKING SODA

½ TEASPOON SALT

1 CUP RAISINS

1 CUP CHOPPED WALNUTS

PREHEAT OVEN TO 375°F (190°C).

Cream butter, shortening and sugar. Blend in apple juice concentrate, egg and spices. Mix in flour, baking soda and salt. Stir in raisins and walnuts. Drop by rounded teaspoonfuls 2 inches apart on ungreased baking sheets. Bake 8 to 10 minutes until lightly browned around edges. Cool 2 minutes, then lift with spatula and transfer to racks.

HOLIDAY HERMITS: Substitute brandy for apple juice concentrate. Substitute ½ cup *each* chopped candied cherries and pineapple for raisins. Substitute chopped toasted pecans for walnuts.

HAWAIIAN HERMITS: Substitute light brown for dark brown sugar. Substitute ¼ cup frozen pineapple juice concentrate for apple juice concentrate. Substitute 1 cup chopped candied pineapple for raisins. Substitute ½ cup each chopped macadamia nuts and toasted coconut for walnuts.

Note: Try storing hermits in tins and keep in the refrigerator. A slice of orange or apple adds flavor to these cookies. Just remember to change the fruit every three days.

These famous giant ginger cookies made a name for themselves in Marblehead, Massachusetts. They remind me of Christmas gingerbread men...only they're perfect for the Fourth of July!

★ ★ ★

GINGER JOE FROGGERS

¹/₂	CUP BUTTER
1	CUP FIRMLY PACKED DARK BROWN SUGAR
1	CUP MOLASSES
¹/₂	CUP WATER OR APPLE JUICE
4	CUPS ALL PURPOSE FLOUR
1¹/₂	TEASPOONS SALT
1	TEASPOON BAKING SODA
1¹/₂	TEASPOONS GINGER
¹/₂	TEASPOON CLOVES
¹/₂	TEASPOON NUTMEG
¹/₄	TEASPOON ALLSPICE
	GRANULATED SUGAR

MAKES
3 dozen

Cream butter and sugar. Blend in molasses and water. In separate bowl, mix all dry ingredients except sugar and blend in to make a soft dough. Wrap dough in plastic and chill until firm.

PREHEAT OVEN TO 375°F (190°C).

Roll out dough ¹/₄ inch thick on floured surface. Cut into 3-inch circles and place 3 inches apart on greased baking sheets. Sprinkle cookies with sugar. Bake for 10 to 12 minutes. Cool on baking sheet for at least 10 minutes before removing with spatula.

I've always loved this recipe for peanut butter cookies, and honey-roasted peanuts make a great addition.

★ ★ ★

HONEY-ROASTED PEANUT BUTTER COOKIES

MAKES

5 dozen

½	CUP (1 stick) BUTTER OR MARGARINE, SOFTENED
½	CUP FIRMLY PACKED LIGHT BROWN SUGAR
½	CUP GRANULATED SUGAR
½	CUP CHUNKY PEANUT BUTTER
1	EGG, BEATEN
1½	CUPS ALL PURPOSE FLOUR
1	TEASPOON BAKING SODA
1	CUP HONEY-ROASTED PEANUTS, COARSELY CHOPPED

PREHEAT OVEN TO 350°F (175°C).

Cream butter, sugars and peanut butter until light and fluffy. Beat in egg, flour and soda to make a smooth dough. Mix in peanuts. Shape dough into 1-inch balls and place 2 inches apart on ungreased baking sheets. Press the back of a fork into each cookie in two directions to make a cross-hatched pattern. Bake 8 to 10 minutes until edges are lightly browned. Cool 10 minutes, then lift cookies with spatula and transfer to racks.

Potato chip cookies?
Believe it. Somewhere,
someone's ingenious mom
invented these for a
school bake sale. What a
brainstorm!

★ ★ ★

IDAHO POTATO TREATS

MAKES
7 dozen

2   CUPS (4 sticks) BUTTER OR MARGARINE

1   CUP FIRMLY PACKED LIGHT BROWN SUGAR

1   TABLESPOON VANILLA EXTRACT

3½   CUPS ALL PURPOSE FLOUR

2½   CUPS COARSELY BROKEN RUFFLED POTATO CHIPS

PREHEAT OVEN TO 350°F (175°C).

Cream butter and sugar. Beat in vanilla and flour. Mix in potato chips. Drop by rounded teaspoonfuls onto ungreased baking sheets. Flatten with fork. Bake for 15 minutes until golden around edges. Cool 10 minutes, then transfer to racks with spatula.

*These are interesting
confections with a
surprising
ingredient...oatmeal!
When stored in a covered
container, they taste like
the richest, creamiest
chocolate truffles. When
allowed to dry out, they're
crisp and fudgy. Either
way, they're delicious.*

★ ★ ★

CHOCOLATE TRUFFETTES

MAKES
3 dozen

2   CUPS SUGAR

½   CUP (1 stick) UNSALTED BUTTER

½   CUP MILK

½   CUP UNSWEETENED COCOA POWDER

2   CUPS QUICK-COOKING ROLLED OATS

2   CUPS CHOPPED TOASTED PECANS OR ALMONDS
    (reserve 1 cup)

1   TEASPOON VANILLA OR ½ TEASPOON ALMOND EXTRACT

Combine sugar, butter and milk in large saucepan and bring to boil
over low heat. Simmer 3 minutes, stirring frequently. Remove from
heat and whisk in cocoa, oatmeal, 1 cup nuts and vanilla. Chill
mixture for about an hour. Shape into 36 balls and roll in remaining
nuts. Refrigerate in covered container or allow to dry at room
temperature.

This unique recipe was the favorite fudge of my fifth-grade class. It's so easy that a child can whip up a batch.

★ ★ ★

PHILADELPHIA "PHUDGE"

MAKES
1-3/4 pounds

4 OUNCES UNSWEETENED CHOCOLATE
1 TABLESPOON UNSALTED BUTTER
  8-OUNCE PACKAGE CREAM CHEESE, SOFTENED
4 CUPS (1 POUND) SIFTED POWDERED SUGAR
1 TABLESPOON VANILLA EXTRACT
1/8 TEASPOON SALT
1/2 CUP TOASTED CHOPPED PECANS (see Note)

Melt chocolate and butter together over low heat (or in microwave); stir until smooth. Beat cream cheese in bowl with mixer until fluffy. Blend in chocolate mixture. Add powdered sugar, vanilla and salt and beat until smooth. Stir in nuts. Spread into 8-inch square pan lined with foil. Chill until firm, then cut into squares.

Note: For the holidays, substitute 1/2 cup chopped candied cherries or 1/3 cup crushed peppermint candy for pecans.

Pumpkin cookies are extremely popular at fall bake sales, tying together the Halloween and Thanksgiving seasons. I love this recipe for the divine penuche glaze. On Halloween, decorate with candy corn for jack o'lantern faces.

★ ★ ★

GREAT PUMPKIN COOKIES

4 dozen

1 CUP (2 sticks) BUTTER OR MARGARINE, SOFTENED

$^{1}/_{2}$ CUP GRANULATED SUGAR

$^{1}/_{2}$ CUP FIRMLY PACKED BROWN SUGAR

1 CUP CANNED PUMPKIN

1 EGG

1 TEASPOON VANILLA EXTRACT

2 CUPS ALL PURPOSE FLOUR

1 TEASPOON BAKING SODA

1 TEASPOON BAKING POWDER

2 TEASPOONS PUMPKIN PIE SPICE

$^{1}/_{4}$ TEASPOON SALT

$^{3}/_{4}$ CUP CHOPPED WALNUTS

Penuche Glaze (recipe follows)

PREHEAT OVEN TO 350°F (175°C).

Cream butter and sugars until light and fluffy. Blend in pumpkin, egg and vanilla. Mix in flour, soda, baking powder, pumpkin pie spice, salt and nuts. Drop by tablespoonfuls 3 inches apart on ungreased baking sheets. Bake 10 to 12 minutes until golden around edges. Lift warm cookies from baking sheet with spatula, and transfer to racks. Cool about 30 minutes, then spread with glaze.

Penuche Glaze

3   TABLESPOONS BUTTER OR MARGARINE
1/2   CUP FIRMLY PACKED DARK BROWN SUGAR
1/4   CUP MILK
1/2 to 2   CUPS POWDERED SUGAR

Heat butter and brown sugar in medium saucepan until bubbly. Cook, stirring constantly, for 1 minute until slightly thickened. Beat in milk. Blend in enough powdered sugar to make glaze a smooth, spreadable consistency.

HALLOWEEN PARTY PUMPKIN COOKIES: Here's a way to entertain little goblins on Halloween night. Bake the cookies in advance and set out bowls of frosting and dishes of candy corn. Kids love making their own trick or treats.

So festive and fun to make. Your kids will love baking these.

★ ★ ★

CANDY CANE COOKIES

½   CUP (1 stick) BUTTER OR MARGARINE, SOFTENED

½   CUP SHORTENING

1   CUP POWDERED SUGAR

1   EGG

1½   TEASPOONS ALMOND EXTRACT

1   TEASPOON VANILLA EXTRACT

2½   CUPS ALL PURPOSE FLOUR

½   TEASPOON SALT

½   TEASPOON RED FOOD COLORING

½   CUP GRANULATED SUGAR

½   CUP CRUSHED PEPPERMINT CANDY

MAKES
4 dozen

PREHEAT OVEN TO 375°F (190°C).

Cream butter, shortening, and powdered sugar. Blend in egg, flavorings, flour, and salt. Divide dough in half; tint one part with red food coloring. For each cookie, shape 1 teaspoon red dough into 4-inch rope. Repeat with 1 teaspoon plain dough. Twist ropes together and shape like a candy cane. Place on ungreased baking sheet. Mix sugar with crushed candy. Bake cookies about 9 minutes until set and *very lightly* browned. Immediately sprinkle with candy mixture. Gently remove hot cookies from baking sheet with spatula.

Also known as "Mexican wedding cakes" and "pecan balls," these are always a big hit during the holidays...so why not enjoy them year-round? Try a few of these nutty nuggets on a hot summer afternoon, alongside a dish of butter pecan ice cream.

★ ★ ★

NUTCRACKER NUGGETS

MAKES 4 dozen

1	CUP (2 sticks) BUTTER OR MARGARINE, SOFTENED
1/2	CUP POWDERED SUGAR
2	TEASPOONS VANILLA EXTRACT
2	CUPS ALL PURPOSE FLOUR
1 1/2	CUPS FINELY CHOPPED TOASTED PECANS
	POWDERED SUGAR

Cream butter, 1/2 cup powdered sugar and vanilla until light and fluffy. Mix in flour and nuts to make a soft dough. Cover with plastic wrap and chill 2 hours.

PREHEAT OVEN TO 350°F (175°C).

Shape dough into 3/4-inch balls and place 1 inch apart on ungreased baking sheet. Bake 12 to 14 minutes or until pale brown. Remove from oven and roll warm cookies in powdered sugar. Cool, then roll again in powdered sugar.

These always make a beautiful addition to an assortment of Christmas cookies.

★ ★ ★

THUMBPRINTS

³/₄ CUP (1¹/₂ sticks) BUTTER OR MARGARINE, SOFTENED

$^1/_2$ CUP SUGAR

1 EGG

1 TEASPOON VANILLA EXTRACT

$^1/_2$ TEASPOON ALMOND EXTRACT

2 CUPS ALL PURPOSE FLOUR

1 TEASPOON BAKING POWDER

$^1/_4$ TEASPOON SALT

1 TEASPOON GRATED ORANGE OR LEMON PEEL

1$^1/_2$ CUPS CHOPPED TOASTED ALMONDS (reserve 1 cup)

Thick raspberry, apricot or boysenberry preserves (see Note)

MAKES
4 dozen

PREHEAT OVEN TO 350°F (175°C).

Cream butter and sugar. Beat in egg and extracts. Mix in dry ingredients, grated peel and ½ cup almonds. Shape dough into 4 dozen balls and roll in remaining almonds. Place balls 2 inches apart on greased cookie sheets. Make a deep indentation in the center of each ball. Bake 10 minutes. Fill centers with dabs of preserves and return to oven for about 3 minutes to set. Cool completely before lifting with spatula.

Note: To make thick preserves, heat a jar of jam until liquid. Pour into strainer to let excess juice drain from fruit pulp. Cool to room temperature before using.

Opposite: Country Fair Caramel Apple Cakes, page 164

A cookie gun is an indispensable piece of equipment for holiday baking.

★ ★ ★

SUGARPLUM SPRITZ

MAKES
6 dozen

1   CUP (2 sticks) BUTTER OR MARGARINE, SOFTENED

1   CUP SUGAR

1   EGG

½   TEASPOON ALMOND EXTRACT

2¼   CUPS ALL PURPOSE FLOUR

⅛   TEASPOON SALT

  Candied fruit: red and green cherry halves, pineapple cubes, pieces of apricot

PREHEAT OVEN TO 400°F (200°C).

Cream butter and sugar. Blend in egg and almond extract. Mix in flour, salt and almond extract to make a smooth dough. Pack dough in batches into cookie gun or press. Press out desired shapes onto ungreased cookie sheets. Press fruits lightly into centers of cookies. Bake 7 to 8 minutes until set. Cool, then remove from cookie sheets.

Opposite: Carrot Bread, page 171; Zucchini Bread, page 171; Waldorf Apple Bread, page 172

(Sand Tarts, Christmas Cutouts, Sweet Hearts)

A basic crisp sugar cookie dough you'll want to use year-round for cut-out cookies.

★ ★ ★

SUGAR COOKIE CLASSICS

MAKES
4 dozen

$^1/_2$ CUP (1 stick) BUTTER OR MARGARINE, SOFTENED

1 CUP SUGAR

1 EGG

$1^3/_4$ CUPS ALL PURPOSE FLOUR

$^1/_4$ TEASPOON SALT

1 TEASPOON VANILLA OR $^1/_2$ TEASPOON ALMOND EXTRACT

PREHEAT OVEN TO 325°F (160°C).

Cream butter and sugar until light and fluffy. Beat in egg. Mix in flour, salt and vanilla to make a smooth dough. Roll dough out $^1/_8$ inch thick on well-floured surface and prepare in any of the ways suggested below. Bake 8 minutes until set and pale brown. Lift cookies off sheet with spatula while still warm.

SAND TARTS: Cut dough into $2^1/_2$-inch rounds. Place on greased cookie sheets about 1 inch apart. Stir together egg white and 1 teaspoon water with fork. Brush over tops of cookies. Sprinkle with cinnamon sugar. Press whole almond in center of each.

CHRISTMAS CUTOUTS: Use holiday cutters to cut desired shapes. Sprinkle with colored sugar before baking.

SWEET HEARTS: Cut dough into heart shapes and bake. When cooled, sandwich hearts back to back with 1 teaspoon strawberry or raspberry jam.

PARADE OF PIES

NEVER-FAIL PIECRUST • MAGIC MAYONNAISE PIECRUST

CHEESY APPLE PIZZA • PEACH BERRY PIE • BLUEBERRY BUCKLE PIE

CRANBERRY PEAR PIE • OLD-FASHIONED FRESH CHERRY PIE

LOUISIANA BANANA PECAN PIE • KEY LARGO LIME TART • CHARLESTON LEMON CHESS PIE

"HONEY PIE" • KENTUCKY DERBY PIE • SHAKER SUGAR PIE • JAPANESE FRUIT PIE

BUTTERMILK PIE • PILGRIM PUMPKIN PIE • SWEET POTATO PRALINE PIE

GERMAN CHOCOLATE PIE • IMPOSSIBLE "IDIOT" PIE • CRACKEROON PIE

CLASSIC PECAN TASSIES

PARADE OF PIES

Portable pies are by far the most practical kind for bringing to bake sales. Chiffon and cream pies are usually too perishable to hold up without refrigeration. Although some meringue pies don't spoil quite as easily, they can be "weepy" and temperamental on humid days.

So what pies are portable? Freshly baked fruit pies (like mom's apple) will always be appealing. Chess-type pies, really a whole family of rich, sugary custard pies, are also a good choice. Pecan is probably the most popular (although walnut "derby" pie is starting to run neck-and-neck), followed by coconut and lemon chess pies. Tarts and tassies are little pick-up pies, perfect for one person. Full-size or bite-size, when pies are featured at a bake sale, they disappear fast!

PIE POINTERS

TRANSPORTING: You'll notice that there are no chiffon, cream or meringue pies in this section. That's not because they aren't delicious — but they spoil easily and simply don't travel well to bake sales, picnics or parties. Chiffon pies melt. Cream pies invite food poisoning and meringue pies are a mess (when they aren't weeping from humidity, they're stuck to the car seat!). Fruit and chess-type custard pies are much less temperamental.

BAKING: Most pies are best baked on the lower oven rack. This allows the bottom crust to set up and brown before the hot filling can cause it to become soggy. Cover edges of piecrust with strips of foil and remove during the last 10 minutes of baking; this will prevent burning.

COOLING: Never wrap a hot pie in plastic wrap or foil; this will cause the crust to get soggy. Pies should only be covered after they're completely cool. Never cut a pie before it's time! Always wait until fruit or custard fillings have set or you'll end up with a runny, ruined pie. Individual slices (or an entire pie) can then be heated later on, if you wish to serve it warm.

A NOTE ABOUT PIECRUST

Many people shy away from pie baking because they claim you have to "cut their crust with an axe." This happens when pastry is overhandled and the gluten in the flour is developed.

Do you usually end up dusting the whole kitchen floor during a pie project? Then try oil- or mayonnaise-type pastry. This can be rolled out easily between sheets of plastic wrap and is excellent for single-crust pie shells.

It's no great shame if you hate making piecrust from scratch…join the club! Why else do you think there are so many excellent frozen and refrigerated crusts available? (Everyone knows the fun is in the filling.) Just defrost and recrimp the edges. No one will ever notice you "cheated"—and if they do, it's because they do, too!

But for those fruit pie fanciers who insist on "from scratch" crust, the Never-Fail Piecrust is for you. Egg and vinegar make the pastry easy and foolproof to handle.

For those who like making pies the hard way, this recipe makes it easier. Egg and vinegar are its secret to success. This pastry works particularly well with double-crust fruit pies. It's a large recipe, so divide finished dough into 4 balls and wrap in plastic until needed.

★ ★ ★

NEVER-FAIL PIECRUST

3 CUPS ALL PURPOSE FLOUR

1 TEASPOON SALT

1½ CUPS SHORTENING (try using butter-flavored!)

1 EGG

1 TABLESPOON VINEGAR

5 TABLESPOONS ICE WATER

MAKES

two 9-inch

double crusts

or

four 9-inch pie

shells

Combine flour and salt in large bowl and cut in shortening until mixture resembles fine crumbs. Beat egg, vinegar, and water together in glass measuring cup. Pour over flour mixture and stir with fork until blended. Divide into 4 balls. Roll out on floured surface.

Note: To store leftover pie crust, wrap unused balls of pastry in plastic wrap. Keep in refrigerator until needed (up to 2 weeks). May be frozen for 2 months. For best results, defrost frozen pastry balls overnight in the refrigerator.

Mayonnaise pastry is so easy, you simply can't mess it up!

★ ★ ★

MAGIC MAYONNAISE PIECRUST

1   PINT (2 cups) REAL MAYONNAISE

2   TABLESPOONS WATER

2   CUPS ALL PURPOSE FLOUR

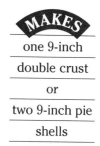

MAKES

one 9-inch

double crust

or

two 9-inch pie

shells

Blend mayonnaise and water in bowl. Stir in flour with fork until mixture forms a ball. Divide in half; shape each half into ball. Roll out each ball on floured surface or between sheets of plastic wrap.

Note: To transfer pastry from plastic wrap to pie plate, peel off top sheet of plastic wrap and invert dough over pie plate, holding onto back sheet of plastic. Gently ease pastry into plate and peel away plastic wrap from back. Crimp edges.

A recent innovation on the bake sale scene. This "pizza" pie is like a large tart laden with grated cheese and streusel topping. It's frequently sold by the slice.

★ ★ ★

CHEESY APPLE PIZZA

7   MEDIUM-SIZE TART APPLES, CORED AND THINLY SLICED (do not peel)

$^1\!/_2$ CUP SUGAR

1   TEASPOON CINNAMON

$^1\!/_4$ TEASPOON NUTMEG

1   CUP GRATED SHARP CHEDDAR CHEESE

    Streusel Crumb Topping (recipe follows)

    Pastry for double-crust pie (try using $^1\!/_2$ recipe of Never-fail Piecrust)

MAKES
one 14-inch
pizza

PREHEAT OVEN TO 425°F (230°C).

Form pastry dough into large ball. Roll out into 15- to 16-inch circle and ease into 14-inch round pizza pan. Pinch up crust edges to form smooth, uncrimped rim resembling a pizza's. Cover crust with rows of overlapping apple slices. Combine sugar and spices and sprinkle over apple slices. Scatter cheese evenly over top. Sprinkle with streusel topping. Bake 30 to 38 minutes until edges are golden brown. This is best served warm.

Streusel Topping

³/₄ CUP ALL PURPOSE FLOUR

¹/₂ CUP SUGAR

¹/₂ CUP (1 stick) COLD BUTTER, CUT INTO CUBES

Mix flour and sugar in bowl. Using pastry blender, cut in butter until mixture forms coarse crumbs.

SERVING TIP: This is a big hit at bake sales when you have access to an electrical outlet. Bring a portable microwave and serve hot apple pizza by the slice.

The combination of fresh peaches and raspberries is a lot like Peach Melba. A good seller at hot August bake sales.

★ ★ ★

PEACH BERRY PIE

5   CUPS SLICED RIPE FREESTONE PEACHES
1   CUP FRESH RASPBERRIES
3/4 CUP SUGAR
3   TABLESPOONS QUICK-COOKING TAPIOCA
2   TABLESPOONS (1/4 stick) MELTED BUTTER
    PINCH OF MACE
    Pastry for double-crust pie (try using 1/2 recipe of Never-fail
    Piecrust)

one 9-inch pie

PREHEAT OVEN TO 425°F (220°C).

Toss fruit, sugar, tapioca, butter and mace in mixing bowl until fruit is well coated. Roll out half of pastry and fit into 9-inch pie pan. Fill pastry crust with fruit mixture. Roll out remaining ball of pastry and ease over filling. Trim and crimp edges. Cut slashes in top crust. Bake 25 minutes. Reduce heat to 350°F (175°C) and bake 25 minutes longer. Let cool at least 1 hour before cutting.

An oatmeal crumb topping spiced with nutmeg really complements Maine blueberries.

★ ★ ★

BLUEBERRY BUCKLE PIE

one 9-inch pie

5 to 6 CUPS FRESH BLUEBERRIES

1 CUP SUGAR

3 TABLESPOONS QUICK-COOKING TAPIOCA

9-inch unbaked pie shell

Oatmeal Buckle (recipe follows)

PREHEAT OVEN TO 425°F (220°C).

Toss blueberries in mixing bowl with sugar and tapioca. Spoon into pie shell. Sprinkle oatmeal topping evenly over blueberries. Bake 25 minutes. Reduce heat to 350°F (175°C) and bake 25 minutes longer. Let cool at least 1 hour before cutting.

Oatmeal Buckle

$1/4$ CUP ($1/2$ stick) BUTTER, CUT INTO CUBES

$1/2$ CUP FIRMLY PACKED LIGHT BROWN SUGAR

$1/3$ CUP ALL PURPOSE FLOUR

$1/3$ CUP QUICK-COOKING ROLLED OATS

$1/2$ TEASPOON CINNAMON

$1/2$ TEASPOON NUTMEG

Using pastry blender, mix all ingredients until crumbly.

Variations ★ ★ ★ ★ ★ ★ ★ ★ ★ ★ ★ ★ ★ ★ ★ ★ ★

Try substituting fresh blackberries, boysenberries, even huckle-berries, for blueberries. Any version is divine with softened vanilla ice cream, spiced with a dash of nutmeg.

Combining the sweetness of maple syrup and the tart touch of cranberries, this pie has a real New England flavor. It makes a refreshing addition to the holiday pie lineup.

★ ★ ★

CRANBERRY PEAR PIE

MAKES
one 9-inch pie

5   CUPS CORED, THINLY SLICED PEARS

1   CUP FRESH CRANBERRIES

1/2   CUP MAPLE SYRUP

2   TABLESPOONS ALL PURPOSE FLOUR

2   TABLESPOONS (1/4 stick) MELTED BUTTER

    9-inch unbaked pie shell

    Crumb Topping (recipe follows)

PREHEAT OVEN TO 400°F (200°C).

Combine pears, cranberries, syrup, flour and butter in large bowl. Mix with large spoon or spatula until fruit is evenly coated. Spoon into pie shell. Sprinkle crumb topping over fruit. Bake 15 minutes. Reduce heat to 350°F (175°C) and bake 35 minutes longer, until golden brown. Let cool at least 1 hour before cutting.

Crumb Topping

1/2   CUP ALL PURPOSE FLOUR

1/4   CUP FIRMLY PACKED LIGHT BROWN SUGAR

1   TEASPOON CINNAMON

1/3   CUP COLD BUTTER OR MARGARINE, CUT INTO CUBES

1/2   CUP CHOPPED WALNUTS

Using pastry blender, mix flour, sugar, cinnamon and butter until crumbly. Stir in walnuts.

SERVING IDEA: Try topping this pie with heavy cream that has been sweetened with a touch of maple syrup. Whip just until soft peaks form.

If you can't get a hold of fresh cherries, substitute frozen ones (thawed and drained). A lattice crust is a classic must!

★ ★ ★

OLD-FASHIONED FRESH CHERRY PIE

one 9-inch pie

5 to 6	CUPS FRESH CHERRIES, PITTED
1	CUP SUGAR
3	TABLESPOONS QUICK-COOKING TAPIOCA
2	TABLESPOONS (¹/₄ stick) MELTED BUTTER
¹/₂	TEASPOON ALMOND EXTRACT
	Pastry for double-crust pie (try using ¹/₂ recipe of Never-fail Piecrust)

PREHEAT OVEN TO 425°F (220°C).

Toss cherries, sugar, tapioca, butter and flavoring in bowl until cherries are well coated. Roll out half of pastry and fit into 9-inch pie pan. Spoon cherries into crust. For lattice, roll out second ball of pastry and cut into ¹/₂-inch-wide strips. Weave a lattice top with strips of dough. Trim pastry at edges with 1-inch overhang and crimp edges. Bake 25 minutes. Reduce heat to 350°F (175°C) and bake 25 minutes longer, until golden brown. Let cool at least 1 hour before cutting.

There are many pecan pies, but this one is special. Bananas, cinnamon and rum make this taste like Bananas Foster after a breakfast at Brennan's in New Orleans.

★ ★ ★

LOUISIANA BANANA PECAN PIE

1   LARGE BANANA, CUBED

1   CUP CHOPPED TOASTED PECANS

1   CUP FIRMLY PACKED LIGHT BROWN SUGAR

3   EGGS, BEATEN

$1/2$ CUP LIGHT CORN SYRUP

$1/4$ CUP ($1/2$ stick) MELTED BUTTER

2   TABLESPOONS RUM

1   TEASPOON CINNAMON

$1/4$ TEASPOON SALT

     9-inch unbaked pie shell

MAKES
one 9-inch pie

PREHEAT OVEN TO 375°F (190°C).

Blend all ingredients except crust with spatula and pour into pie shell. Bake 45 minutes, until crust is golden and filling is set. Let cool at least 2 hours before cutting.

Unlike the sweetened condensed milk versions, this one can be kept at room temperature—an important feature for bake sale fare.

★ ★ ★

KEY LARGO LIME TART

MAKES
one 9-inch pie

½	CUP (1 stick) BUTTER
1	CUP SUGAR
1	CUP FRESH LIME JUICE
4	EGG YOLKS
2	EGGS
1	TABLESPOON GRATED LIME PEEL
2	DROPS GREEN FOOD COLORING (optional)
	9-inch pie shell, baked and cooled
½	CUP LIGHTLY TOASTED COCONUT

Melt butter in saucepan over low heat. Whisk in sugar, lime juice, egg yolks, eggs and lime peel and cook, stirring constantly, until mixture thickens. Stir in coloring. Let cool to room temperature. Pour into pie shell. Top with toasted coconut.

*A Southern classic—
sweet, rich and not for the
calorie-shy!*

★ ★ ★

CHARLESTON LEMON CHESS PIE

one 9-inch pie

1 CUP (2 sticks) BUTTER

2 CUPS SUGAR

1 TABLESPOON CORNSTARCH

4 EGGS

2 TEASPOONS GRATED LEMON PEEL

7 TABLESPOONS LEMON JUICE

9-inch unbaked pie shell

PREHEAT OVEN TO 350°F (175°C).

Cream butter, sugar and cornstarch until light and fluffy. Add eggs one at a time, beating well after each addition. Blend in lemon peel and juice. Pour into pie shell. (If using frozen pie shell, defrost and crimp edges very high.) Bake until filling is set, 40 to 45 minutes. Let cool at least 2 hours before cutting.

*A delicious recipe dating
back to the 1920s,
also known as
"Bee's Knees Pie."*

★ ★ ★

"HONEY PIE"

1	CUP TOASTED SLIVERED ALMONDS
1	CUP SUGAR
$^3/_4$	CUP HONEY
3	EGGS, SLIGHTLY BEATEN
$^1/_4$	CUP ($^1/_2$ stick) MELTED BUTTER
2	TABLESPOONS HEAVY CREAM
1	TEASPOON VANILLA EXTRACT
$^1/_2$	TEASPOON ALMOND EXTRACT
$^1/_4$	TEASPOON SALT
	9-inch unbaked pie shell

MAKES
one 9-inch pie

PREHEAT OVEN TO 375°F (190°C).

Blend all ingredients except crust in mixing bowl. Pour into pie shell. Bake 40 to 50 minutes, until crust is set and filling is golden. Let cool at least 2 hours before cutting.

This increasingly popular pie is starting to run neck and neck with pecan pie in bake sales. It's really quite similar, except that it features walnuts and chocolate chips.

KENTUCKY DERBY PIE

one 9-inch pie

1	CUP FIRMLY PACKED LIGHT BROWN SUGAR
3/4	CUP LIGHT CORN SYRUP
3	EGGS, LIGHTLY BEATEN
1/2	CUP SEMISWEET CHOCOLATE CHIPS
1/2	CUP CHOPPED TOASTED WALNUTS
1/4	CUP (1/2 stick) MELTED BUTTER
2	TABLESPOONS BOURBON
1	TEASPOON VANILLA EXTRACT
1/4	TEASPOON SALT
	9-inch unbaked pie shell

PREHEAT OVEN TO 375°F (190°C).

Blend all ingredients except crust in mixing bowl. Pour into pie shell. Bake 40 to 50 minutes, until crust is golden and filling is set. Let cool at least 2 hours before cutting.

PARADE OF PIES

This New England version of chess pie is very homey and humble. Its simplicity is what makes it so sophisticated.

★ ★ ★

SHAKER SUGAR PIE

MAKES
one 9-inch pie

2   EGGS

2   EGG YOLKS

1   CUP SUGAR

1/2   CUP (1 stick) MELTED BUTTER

2   TABLESPOONS HEAVY CREAM

1   TABLESPOON CIDER VINEGAR

1   TABLESPOON VANILLA EXTRACT

1   TABLESPOON WHITE OR YELLOW CORNMEAL

1/2   TEASPOON NUTMEG

9-inch unbaked pie shell

PREHEAT OVEN TO 350°F (175°C).

Beat whole eggs and yolks together in mixing bowl. Blend in sugar, butter, cream, vinegar, vanilla, cornmeal and nutmeg. Pour mixture into pie shell. Bake 35 to 40 minutes, until crust is golden and filling is set. Let cool at least 2 hours before cutting.

111

A wonderful holiday pie, this reminds me of a Southern-style light fruitcake, baked in a crust.

★ ★ ★

JAPANESE FRUIT PIE

1   CUP SUGAR

1/2   CUP (1 stick) MELTED BUTTER OR MARGARINE

1/2   CUP SHREDDED OR FLAKED COCONUT

1/2   CUP GOLDEN RAISINS

1/2   CUP CHOPPED TOASTED PECANS

1/2   CUP CRUSHED PINEAPPLE, *VERY WELL DRAINED*

2   DOZEN CANDIED CHERRIES, HALVED

2   EGGS, BEATEN

1   TEASPOON VANILLA EXTRACT

1   TEASPOON CIDER VINEGAR

     9-inch unbaked pie shell

MAKES
one 9-inch pie

PREHEAT OVEN TO 300°F (150°C).

Blend all ingredients except crust in mixing bowl. Pour into pie shell. Bake about 40 minutes until filling is set. Let cool at least 2 hours before cutting.

This pie shows up at a lot of bake sales in Maryland, Virginia and North Carolina.

★ ★ ★

BUTTERMILK PIE

2 CUPS SUGAR

2 TABLESPOONS ALL PURPOSE FLOUR

2 EGGS, BEATEN

2 CUPS BUTTERMILK

¹/₂ TEASPOON LEMON EXTRACT

9-inch unbaked pie shell

MAKES
one 9-inch pie

PREHEAT OVEN TO 350°F (175°C).

Blend all ingredients except crust in mixing bowl. Pour into pie shell and bake 40 minutes, until crust is golden and filling is set. Let cool at least 3 hours before cutting.

Dark, spicy and maple-flavored...very New England!

★ ★ ★

PILGRIM PUMPKIN PIE

1½ CUPS CANNED PUMPKIN

1 CUP HEAVY CREAM

¾ CUP FIRMLY PACKED DARK BROWN SUGAR

2 EGGS, BEATEN

½ CUP MAPLE SYRUP

2 TEASPOONS PUMPKIN PIE SPICE

9-inch unbaked pie shell

1 CUP BROKEN WALNUT HALVES

2 TABLESPOONS MAPLE SYRUP

MAKES
one 9-inch pie

PREHEAT OVEN TO 425°F (220°C).

Blend pumpkin, cream, sugar, eggs, ½ cup maple syrup and spice in mixing bowl. Pour into pie shell. Sprinkle walnuts over filling. Bake 40 minutes. Remove from oven and brush with 2 tablespoons maple syrup. Return to oven for 5 minutes or until filling is set. Let cool at least 2 hours before cutting.

This Southern cousin to pumpkin pie shows up at the same holiday events. A brown sugar–pecan crust bakes into a praline candy confection.

★ ★ ★

SWEET POTATO PRALINE PIE

3 TABLESPOONS BUTTER OR MARGARINE, SOFTENED

⅓ CUP FIRMLY PACKED DARK BROWN SUGAR

⅓ CUP CHOPPED TOASTED PECANS

9-inch unbaked pie shell

Sweet Potato Filling (recipe follows)

MAKES
one 9-inch pie

PREHEAT OVEN TO 450°F (230°C).

Cream butter and sugar. Blend in pecans. Press into bottom of pie shell. Bake 10 minutes. Remove from oven and let cool slightly while preparing filling.

Reduce heat to 350°F (175°C). Pour filling into crust. Return pie to oven and bake 50 minutes. Let cool at least 2 hours before cutting.

Sweet Potato Filling

2   CUPS MASHED COOKED SWEET POTATOES

1   CUP FIRMLY PACKED LIGHT BROWN SUGAR

1   CUP MILK

½   CUP (1 stick) MELTED BUTTER OR MARGARINE

2   EGGS, BEATEN

2   TABLESPOONS BOURBON (optional)

1   TEASPOON CINNAMON

½   TEASPOON ALLSPICE

½   TEASPOON CLOVES

Blend all ingredients in mixing bowl until smooth.

Note: When pre-baking a pie crust, always be sure to gently ease the pastry into the pan. Stretching a pie crust can cause it to shrink and puff up in the oven.

PARADE OF PIES

A rich pie, chock full of pecans and chewy coconut. It will remind you of German chocolate cake.

★ ★ ★

GERMAN CHOCOLATE PIE

MAKES one 9-inch pie

1   CUP GRANULATED SUGAR

½   CUP FIRMLY PACKED LIGHT BROWN SUGAR

¼   CUP COCOA POWDER

½   CUP EVAPORATED MILK

½   CUP CHOPPED TOASTED PECANS

½   CUP SHREDDED COCONUT

2   EGGS, BEATEN

¼   CUP (½ stick) MELTED BUTTER

  9-inch unbaked pie shell

PREHEAT OVEN TO 400°F (200°C).

Blend all ingredients except crust in mixing bowl. Pour into pie shell. Bake 30 to 35 minutes, until filling is set. Let cool, then chill several hours before cutting.

No, this isn't a pie eaten by idiots. In fact, it's really quite a clever recipe, which dates back to the Bisquick box. It seems impossibly easy (a pie that makes its own crust), and anyone can bake it (even an idiot!).

★ ★ ★

IMPOSSIBLE "IDIOT" PIE

$^1/_2$ CUP BISQUICK

$^1/_3$ CUP SUGAR

4   EGGS

2   CUPS MILK

3   TABLESPOONS MELTED BUTTER OR MARGARINE

1   TEASPOON VANILLA EXTRACT

$1^1/_2$ CUPS SHREDDED COCONUT (one $3^1/_2$-ounce can)

MAKES
one 9-inch pie

PREHEAT OVEN TO 400°F (200°C).

Combine Bisquick, sugar, eggs, milk, butter and vanilla in mixing bowl and beat until smooth. Blend in coconut. Pour into greased 9-inch deep-dish pie plate. Bake 35 to 40 minutes, until set. Cool, then refrigerate for easy slicing.

Another pie that makes its own crust. Graham cracker crumbs and coconut bake into a chewy, macaroonlike filling.

★ ★ ★

CRACKEROON PIE

3 EGG WHITES, ROOM TEMPERATURE

1 TEASPOON BAKING POWDER

1/2 TEASPOON CREAM OF TARTAR

1 CUP SUGAR

1 CUP GRAHAM CRACKER CRUMBS

1 CUP CHOPPED TOASTED PECANS

1/2 CUP SHREDDED OR FLAKED COCONUT

1/2 CUP CHOPPED PITTED DATES

MAKES one 9-inch pie

PREHEAT OVEN TO 350°F (175°C).

Beat egg whites with baking powder and cream of tartar until stiff peaks form. Gradually add sugar, beating until stiff and glossy. Gently fold in graham cracker crumbs, pecans, coconut, and dates.

Grease 9-inch pie pan and dust with a spoonful of graham cracker crumbs (shake pan to coat evenly, then turn upside down and tap to remove excess). Spread pie mixture in pan. Bake 35 minutes. Let cool at least 2 hours before cutting.

*These bite-size pecan pies
are a favorite teatime
treat. You'll see a lot of
pecan tassies at bridal
and baby showers, not
just at bake sales.*

★ ★ ★

CLASSIC PECAN TASSIES

³/₄ CUP FIRMLY PACKED DARK BROWN SUGAR

1 EGG, BEATEN

1 TABLESPOON VANILLA EXTRACT

1 CUP CHOPPED TOASTED PECANS

24 PECAN HALVES

Cream Cheese Tartlet Shells (recipe follows)

MAKES
2 dozen
tartlets

PREHEAT OVEN TO 350°F (175°C).

Beat sugar, egg and vanilla in mixing bowl. Stir in chopped pecans.
Drop a teaspoonful of mixture into center of each tartlet shell. Top
with pecan half. Bake 25 minutes. Let cool 10 minutes, then gently
remove from muffin tins.

Opposite: Classic Pecan Tassies, page 120
Overleaf: Chocolate Chip Rocky Road Pizza, page 28

LOUISIANA BANANA
PIE
$1 slice

KENTUCKY DERBY
PIE
$1 slice

Cream Cheese Tartlet Shells

¹/₂ CUP (1 stick) BUTTER OR MARGARINE, SOFTENED

    3-OUNCE PACKAGE CREAM CHEESE, SOFTENED

1   CUP ALL PURPOSE FLOUR

Beat butter with cream cheese until smooth. Blend in flour to form a soft dough. Chill 1 hour. Roll into 2 dozen small balls and press into bottoms and sides of miniature muffin tins.

Variations ★ ★ ★ ★ ★ ★ ★ ★ ★ ★ ★ ★ ★ ★ ★

Try using walnuts, chopped hazlenuts or almonds in place of pecans. The almond version is excellent when you add ¹/₂ teaspoon of almond extract to the cream cheese pastry dough.

Opposite: Key Largo Lime Tart, page 107

Overleaf: Kentucky Derby Pie (foreground), page 110;
   Louisiana Banana Pecan Pie (background), page 106

CAKEWALK

CLASSIC CARROT CAKE • TOMATO SOUP CAKE • SAUERKRAUT CRAZY CAKE

RED DEVIL MAGIC MAYONNAISE CAKE • LAZY DAISY LUNCHBOX CAKE

COFFEE COCOA CANAL CAKE • COLONIAL ORANGE CAKE

VERMONT MAPLE CAKE • LEMON-GLAZED GINGERBREAD • LOUISIANA BANANA CAKE

LUSCIOUS LANE CAKE • PINEAPPLE PARADISE CAKE • APRICOT BRANDY CAKE

STRAWBERRY RHUBARB CAKE • PINEAPPLE "RIGHT-SIDE-UP" CAKES

CHOCOLATE COCA-COLA CAKE • PEANUT BUTTER CUPCAKES

FRUITCAKE CUPS • COCOROON CAKES • COUNTRY FAIR CARAMEL APPLE CAKES

CAKE WALK

Celebrations and special events call for a cake. (Whoever heard of a birthday pie?) But cakes also make those little memories last…like licking your very first frosting bowl. Cakes mark the milestones in life, as well as turning an ordinary day into an occasion.

I'm always in search of those extraordinary cakes that stand out in a crowd. (The ones that beg me to buy them, the ones that bring me back to the same bake sales year after year). Most fascinating to me are cakes with "magical" or "mysterious" ingredients: mayonnaise, tomato soup, even sauerkraut! Amusing? Don't laugh…even the common carrot cake had to get started somewhere. Probably at a bake sale!

CAKE TALK

As with the pies in this book, the cakes were also selected for their popularity and *portability.* Seven-minute and white mountain frostings, like sticky meringue pies, can get messy when moving from one place to another. Sorry, Lord and Lady Baltimore, but I couldn't invite you to a bake sale!

Deciding how you are going to package your cake is probably as important as deciding what to bake. If you're selling it by the slice (or serving it to a crowd), your only real concern is protecting it from harm. Oftentimes, as with sheet cakes, you can just leave it in the pan and lightly cover it with foil or plastic wrap. (Use tooth-picks to prop cover away from frosting.) There are many excellent rubberseal container products for storing fresh layer cakes.

If you are selling the entire cake(s), don't overlook the wonderful array of foil pans with plastic dome lids (see "It's a Wrap") that are now available. These enable you to bake, frost, serve and sell the cake in the same pan. (And there's usually no need to grease or flour these pans.) When you need to package a layer cake, look for cake boards and cardboard boxes from a convenient supplier.

Even though most of these recipes call for greasing and flouring the pans, you can save a lot of time by remembering two words: *baking parchment.* It's the professional baker's secret. Your cake will never stick to the pan again, and cleaning up is a breeze. Not only is the preparation easier (just cut paper to fit pans), but the cakes bake more evenly. The paper reduces burned bottoms and bunched-up tops.

Finally, about baking times: No two ovens are alike. That's why, regardless of the approximate baking times, cake testing is crucial. A toothpick is usually inserted in the center to see if it comes out "clean" (that is, with no gooey batter residue); this is what is meant by a cake testing "done" with a toothpick. In some cases a cake should feel springy to the touch. And then there are those special cases when the cake is supposed to be so dense and rich that you can't test it...with these, you'll just have to trust me!

Even though carrot cakes have been part of our American culture since colonial times, this version is a modern day "megahit." In the '60s a carrot cake was a curiosity. Now it's an obligatory menu item in most restaurants.

★ ★ ★

CLASSIC CARROT CAKE

one
10 x 15-inch
sheet cake

4	EGGS
2	CUPS SUGAR
1½	CUPS VEGETABLE OIL
2	CUPS ALL PURPOSE FLOUR
2	TEASPOONS BAKING SODA
½	TEASPOON SALT
½	TEASPOON CINNAMON
3	CUPS GRATED CARROTS
	8-OUNCE CAN CRUSHED PINEAPPLE, WELL DRAINED
	Cream Cheese Frosting (recipe follows)

PREHEAT OVEN TO 350°F (175°C).

Beat eggs and sugar at high speed of mixer until light, fluffy, and lemon-colored. Add oil in a slow, steady stream, beating well. Blend in dry ingredients, carrots, and pineapple. Pour into greased and floured 10 x 15-inch jelly roll pan. Bake 28 to 33 minutes, until cake is springy to the touch. Let cool completely, then spread with cream cheese frosting.

Cream Cheese Frosting

8-OUNCE PACKAGE CREAM CHEESE, SOFTENED

$^1/_2$ CUP (1 stick) BUTTER OR MARGARINE

1-POUND BOX (about 4 cups) POWDERED SUGAR

2 TEASPOONS VANILLA EXTRACT

$^1/_2$ CUP GOLDEN RAISINS

$^1/_2$ CUP CHOPPED TOASTED PECANS

Beat cream cheese and butter until light and fluffy. Add sugar and vanilla and blend until smooth and creamy. Stir in raisins and pecans.

Variation ★ ★ ★ ★ ★ ★ ★ ★ ★ ★ ★ ★ ★ ★ ★ ★ ★

ZUCCHINI CAKE: Substitute 3 cups grated fresh zucchini, squeezed dry, for carrots.

This is one of those "novelty" cakes, along with mayonnaise cake, sauerkraut cake and zucchini cake. It's delicious and a real conversation piece.

★ ★ ★

TOMATO SOUP CAKE

MAKES

one 9-inch

layer cake

³/₄	CUP (1¹/₂ sticks) BUTTER OR MARGARINE
1	CUP SUGAR
1	EGG
2¹/₂	CUPS ALL PURPOSE FLOUR
2	TEASPOONS BAKING POWDER
¹/₂	TEASPOON BAKING SODA
1¹/₂	TEASPOONS CINNAMON
1	TEASPOON ALLSPICE
1	TEASPOON CLOVES
1	CAN (10³/₄ ounces) CONDENSED TOMATO SOUP
1	CUP GOLDEN RAISINS
1	CUP CHOPPED WALNUTS
	White Gold Frosting (recipe follows)

PREHEAT OVEN TO 350°F (175°C).

Cream butter and sugar until smooth. Beat in egg. Blend in dry ingredients and tomato soup. Stir in raisins and walnuts. Spray two 9-inch round pans with nonstick coating. Spoon batter into pans and bake 30-35 minutes, until golden brown and springy to touch. Let cakes cool completely. Assemble with frosting.

White Gold Frosting

½ CUP (1 stick) BUTTER OR MARGARINE, SOFTENED

3-OUNCE PACKAGE CREAM CHEESE, SOFTENED

3 CUPS POWDERED SUGAR

1 to 2 TABLESPOONS LEMON JUICE

Beat butter and cream cheese until light and fluffy. Blend in powdered sugar and enough lemon juice to make a spreadable frosting.

Note: If your kids recoil at the thought of tomatoes for dessert, remind them that a tomato is a fruit, not a vegetable. Once they've tasted tomato soup cake, you'll have to convince them that it still isn't o.k. to eat cake for dinner!

Although this cake has a traditional Pennsylvania Dutch origin, its popularity probably grew as a practical joke. My brother ran away screaming from a sauerkraut cake! Later on, I tricked him into trying it. He then devoured two slices of the "best chocolate macaroon cake" he'd ever tasted.

★ ★ ★

SAUERKRAUT CRAZY CAKE

one 9 x 13-inch sheet cake

$1/2$	CUP (1 stick) BUTTER OR MARGARINE, SOFTENED
$1^1/_2$	CUPS SUGAR
3	EGGS
1	TEASPOON ALMOND EXTRACT (or vanilla, if preferred)
$1/2$	CUP UNSWEETENED COCOA POWDER
1	CUP BUTTERMILK
2	CUPS ALL PURPOSE FLOUR
1	TEASPOON BAKING POWDER
1	TEASPOON BAKING SODA
1	CUP SAUERKRAUT, DRAINED, RINSED AND SNIPPED WITH SCISSORS
	Chocolate Glaze (recipe follows)

PREHEAT OVEN TO 350°F (175°C).

Cream butter and sugar until smooth. Add eggs one at a time, beating until light and fluffy. Beat in flavoring, cocoa and buttermilk. Blend in dry ingredients and stir in sauerkraut. Pour into greased and floured 9 x 13-inch pan. Bake 35 to 40 minutes, until cake tests done with toothpick. Let cool completely, then spread with chocolate glaze.

Chocolate Glaze

½	CUP (1 stick) BUTTER OR MARGARINE
	3-OUNCES UNSWEETENED CHOCOLATE
3	CUPS POWDERED SUGAR
1	TEASPOON VANILLA EXTRACT
½	TEASPOON ALMOND EXTRACT
3 to 5	TABLESPOONS HOT WATER

Melt butter and chocolate in medium saucepan over low heat, whisking until smooth. Whisk in powdered sugar, flavorings and enough hot water to make a creamy glaze.

Note: Be sure to rinse the sauerkraut well so that you remove any "briney" taste. A simple way to chop sauerkraut is to place it in a small, narrow bowl and snip it with scissors.

CAKE WALK

This novelty cake of the 1950s became a popular conversation-piece dessert. Mayonnaise replaces eggs and oil in the recipe, making it as easy as a cake mix. No wonder this is enjoying a renaissance. Try it with a cocoa fudge frosting or, German chocolate cake–style, with coconut pecan frosting.

★ ★ ★

RED DEVIL MAGIC MAYONNAISE CAKE

2   CUPS ALL PURPOSE FLOUR

1   CUP REAL MAYONNAISE

1   CUP SUGAR

1   CUP COLD WATER (or cold coffee for a mocha-flavored cake)

1/3   CUP UNSWEETENED COCOA POWDER

2   TEASPOONS VANILLA EXTRACT

2   TEASPOONS BAKING SODA

1/2   TEASPOON SALT

Devil's Food Fudge Frosting or Coconut Pecan Frosting (recipes follow)

MAKES
one 8-inch
layer cake

PREHEAT OVEN TO 350°F (175°C).

Combine all cake ingredients in bowl and whisk until very smooth. Pour into two greased and floured 8-inch round pans. Bake 25 to 30 minutes, until toothpick inserted in center comes out clean. Let cool 5 minutes in pan, then turn out and cool completely on wire racks. Fill and frost top and sides with fudge frosting, or fill and frost tops of layers with coconut pecan frosting.

Devil's Food Fudge Frosting

3 CUPS POWDERED SUGAR

$^{1}/_{2}$ CUP UNSWEETENED COCOA POWDER

$^{1}/_{2}$ CUP (1 stick) BUTTER OR MARGARINE, SOFTENED

3 TABLESPOONS WATER OR COLD, STRONG COFFEE

1 TEASPOON VANILLA EXTRACT

Combine all ingredients in bowl and beat until smooth and creamy.

Coconut Pecan Frosting

$^{2}/_{3}$ CUP EVAPORATED MILK OR LIGHT CREAM

$^{2}/_{3}$ CUP FIRMLY PACKED LIGHT BROWN SUGAR

$^{1}/_{4}$ CUP ($^{1}/_{2}$ stick) BUTTER OR MARGARINE

1 EGG, LIGHTLY BEATEN

1 CUP SHREDDED COCONUT

$^{1}/_{2}$ CUP CHOPPED TOASTED PECANS

$^{1}/_{2}$ TEASPOON VANILLA EXTRACT

Combine milk, sugar, butter and egg in saucepan over medium heat. Cook, stirring, until thickened and bubbly. Blend in coconut, pecans and vanilla. Let cool until thick enough to spread.

CAKE WALK

This oatmeal cake is popular for picnic lunches because of its nice, neat, broiled-on frosting. It's also a snap to make for "lazy" bakers.

★ ★ ★

LAZY DAISY LUNCHBOX CAKE

MAKES
one 9 x 13-inch
sheet cake

1½	CUPS BOILING WATER
1	CUP QUICK-COOKING ROLLED OATS
½	CUP (1 stick) BUTTER OR MARGARINE, SOFTENED
1	CUP GRANULATED SUGAR
2	EGGS, LIGHTLY BEATEN
1	TEASPOON VANILLA EXTRACT
1⅓	CUPS ALL PURPOSE FLOUR
½	TEASPOON BAKING SODA
¼	TEASPOON SALT
1	CUP FIRMLY PACKED LIGHT BROWN SUGAR
1	TEASPOON CINNAMON
½	TEASPOON NUTMEG
	Broiled Frosting (recipe follows)

Pour boiling water over oats, butter and granulated sugar. Let stand 20 minutes.

PREHEAT OVEN TO 350°F (175°C).

Add eggs, vanilla and dry ingredients to oat mixture, stirring to blend. Pour into greased and floured 9 x 13-inch pan. Bake 35 minutes. Spread frosting over cake and broil until lightly browned.

Broiled Frosting

$^1/_2$ CUP (1 stick) MELTED BUTTER OR MARGARINE

$^3/_4$ CUP FIRMLY PACKED LIGHT BROWN SUGAR

$^1/_4$ CUP EVAPORATED MILK OR LIGHT CREAM

1 CUP SHREDDED COCONUT

1 CUP CHOPPED WALNUTS

1 TEASPOON VANILLA EXTRACT

Combine all ingredients in saucepan or bowl.

BROILING TIP: Ovens are not created equal. They usually have hot and cold spots. When broiling the frosting, watch the cake carefully. Rotate the pan if necessary, to assure even browning.

Tube cakes with whirling-twirling centers or a ring of filling running through them took the '60s by storm. The biggest rage was a Bundt cake with ribbons of chocolate fudge. My favorite starts with a rich mocha pound cake. Slice thin and this can easily serve 24.

★ ★ ★

COFFEE COCOA CANAL CAKE

one 10-inch
tube cake

1	CUP (2 sticks) BUTTER OR MARGARINE, SOFTENED
8	OUNCE PACKAGE CREAM CHEESE, SOFTENED
1	TABLESPOON INSTANT COFFEE (not freeze-dried)
6	TABLESPOONS UNSWEETENED COCOA POWDER
1/2	CUP FIRMLY PACKED DARK BROWN SUGAR
1	CUP GRANULATED SUGAR
1	TEASPOON VANILLA EXTRACT
4	EGGS
2 1/4	CUPS ALL PURPOSE FLOUR
1 1/2	TEASPOONS BAKING POWDER
	Pecan Fudge Filling (recipe follows)
	Mocha Fudge Glaze (recipe follows)

PREHEAT OVEN TO 325°F (160°C).

Grease and flour a 10-inch Bundt pan. With electric mixer, cream butter, cream cheese, coffee, cocoa, brown sugar, granulated sugar, and vanilla extract until fluffy. Add eggs, beating well after each. Combine flour and baking powder in separate bowl, then mix into batter. Beat on medium speed for 3 minutes. Spread half of batter in the pan. Drop teaspoonfuls of filling around the pan, running through the batter. Cover with remaining batter. Bake for 70 to 75 minutes, until toothpick inserted in center comes out clean. Let cool, then invert onto plate. Spread glaze on all sides of the cake.

Pecan Fudge Filling

$^1/_4$ CUP ($^1/_2$ stick) BUTTER OR MARGARINE, SOFTENED

$^1/_4$ CUP COCOA POWDER

  1 TEASPOON INSTANT COFFEE (not freeze-dried)

$^3/_4$ CUP FIRMLY PACKED DARK BROWN SUGAR

  1 TEASPOON VANILLA EXTRACT

  1 CUP TOASTED PECANS, COARSELY CHOPPED

Blend butter, cocoa, coffee, sugar, and vanilla together in a bowl. Mix in pecans.

Mocha Fudge Glaze

$^1/_4$ CUP COCOA POWDER

  1 CUP POWDERED SUGAR

  1 TEASPOON INSTANT COFFEE (not freeze-dried)

  1 TABLESPOON BUTTER, SOFTENED

3 to 5 TABLESPOONS VERY HOT WATER

Blend cocoa, powdered sugar, coffee, and butter together with enough of the hot water to make a smooth glaze. Stir well.

This cake has its roots around the Williamsburg, Virginia region, where it still shows up at community gatherings. The creamy, not-too-sweet orange frosting predates the time when powdered sugar was plentiful. The electric mixer makes a breeze out of what must have been a very time-consuming cake.

★ ★ ★

COLONIAL ORANGE CAKE

2½	CUPS ALL PURPOSE FLOUR
1½	CUPS SUGAR
1½	CUPS BUTTERMILK
3	EGGS
½	CUP (1 stick) BUTTER OR MARGARINE, SOFTENED
¼	CUP VEGETABLE OIL
1½	TEASPOONS VANILLA EXTRACT
1½	TEASPOON BAKING SODA
¾	TEASPOON SALT
1	CUP GOLDEN RAISINS
½	CUP FINELY CHOPPED PECANS
2	TABLESPOONS GRATED ORANGE PEEL
	Colonial Orange Frosting (recipe follows)

MAKES
one 9-inch
layer cake

PREHEAT OVEN TO 350°F (175°C).

Combine flour, sugar, buttermilk, eggs, butter, oil, vanilla, soda and salt in large mixing bowl and beat 3 minutes at high speed. Stir in raisins, pecans and orange peel. Pour into two greased and floured 9-inch round pans. Bake 30 to 35 minutes, until toothpick inserted in center comes out clean. Cool in pans 10 minutes. Remove from pans and cool completely on wire racks. Fill and frost tops of layers with frosting.

Colonial Orange Frosting

$^1/_3$ CUP ALL PURPOSE FLOUR

1 TABLESPOON GRATED ORANGE PEEL

1 CUP MILK

1 CUP (2 sticks) BUTTER OR MARGARINE, SOFTENED

1 CUP SUGAR

1 TEASPOON VANILLA EXTRACT

1 TABLESPOON ORANGE LIQUEUR

Combine flour, orange peel and milk in saucepan and cook over medium heat, stirring until thick and smooth. Let cool to room temperature. Cream butter and sugar with mixer until light and fluffy. Beat in vanilla and orange liqueur. Pour cooled milk mixture into butter cream and continue beating at medium to high speed until creamy smooth and very fluffy, about 5 minutes.

Note: This cake is lovely when garnished with strips of candied orange peel.

I bought a slice of this classic maple syrup sheet cake in Woodstock, Vermont. After the first bite, I knew I'd have to include the recipe in this book.

★ ★ ★

VERMONT MAPLE CAKE

2 CUPS ALL PURPOSE FLOUR

1 TABLESPOON BAKING POWDER

3/4 TEASPOON SALT

2 EGGS

1 CUP MAPLE SYRUP

1 CUP HEAVY CREAM

1/4 CUP (1/2 stick) MELTED BUTTER

Maple Butter Frosting (recipe follows)

2/3 CUP CHOPPED TOASTED WALNUTS

MAKES

one 9 x 13-inch

sheet cake

PREHEAT OVEN TO 350°F (175°C).

Combine flour, baking powder, and salt in medium bowl. Beat eggs in large bowl until thick and lemon-colored. Add maple syrup in a thin stream and continue beating until light and fluffy. Add cream and beat 1 minute longer. Fold in dry ingredients and melted butter until blended. Pour batter into greased and floured 9 x 13-inch pan. Bake 35 to 40 minutes, until toothpick inserted in center comes out clean. Cool completely. Spread with frosting and sprinkle with walnuts.

Maple Butter Frosting

¹/₄   CUP (¹/₂ stick) BUTTER OR MARGARINE, SOFTENED

2   CUPS POWDERED SUGAR

¹/₃   CUP MAPLE SYRUP

Cream butter and sugar until smooth. Add maple syrup and beat until creamy and of spreading consistency.

Note: Do not substitute "light" maple syrup for regular maple syrup. Light syrups are 50 percent water. Commercial syrups (which are based on corn syrup) are actually preferable to "pure" maple syrup in this recipe.

I'm a big fan of gingerbread soaking in a traditional tart lemon sauce. However, this isn't the most practical way to sell it at a bake sale (or serve it at a picnic). This version, glazed with lemon icing, is just as satisfying and much more convenient.

★ ★ ★

LEMON-GLAZED GINGERBREAD

one 9 x 13-inch sheet cake

2   CUPS ALL PURPOSE FLOUR

1   CUP FIRMLY PACKED LIGHT BROWN SUGAR

2   EGGS

1/2 CUP (1 stick) MELTED BUTTER

1/2 CUP VEGETABLE OIL

1   CUP MOLASSES

1   CUP BUTTERMILK

1   TEASPOON VANILLA EXTRACT

4   TEASPOONS CINNAMON

2   TEASPOONS GINGER

1   TEASPOON NUTMEG

1   TEASPOON BAKING SODA

1   TEASPOON SALT

    Lemon Glaze (recipe follows)

PREHEAT OVEN TO 325°F (160°C).

Combine all ingredients except glaze in mixing bowl and beat 2 minutes at medium speed. Pour batter into greased and floured 9 x 13-inch pan. Bake 40 to 50 minutes or until top of cake springs back when lightly touched. Remove from oven and let cool completely. Spread with lemon glaze.

Lemon Glaze

3   CUPS POWDERED SUGAR

2   TABLESPOONS (¼ stick) MELTED BUTTER

¼   CUP FRESH LEMON JUICE

1   TABLESPOON GRATED LEMON PEEL

Blend all ingredients until smooth and creamy. If glaze is too thick, dilute with a little milk.

Variation ★ ★ ★ ★ ★ ★ ★ ★ ★ ★ ★ ★ ★ ★ ★ ★ ★ ★

Try making an orange glaze by substituting orange juice and peel for lemon juice.

A New Orleans–inspired banana cake that features a praline pecan topping.

★ ★ ★

LOUISIANA BANANA CAKE

³/₄ CUP FIRMLY PACKED DARK BROWN SUGAR

¹/₃ CUP BUTTER OR MARGARINE, SOFTENED

3 MEDIUM-SIZE RIPE BANANAS, MASHED

¹/₄ CUP BUTTERMILK

2 TABLESPOONS RUM

1 EGG

1¹/₄ CUPS ALL PURPOSE FLOUR

1 TEASPOON BAKING POWDER

¹/₂ TEASPOON BAKING SODA

¹/₂ TEASPOON SALT

¹/₂ TEASPOON CINNAMON

¹/₈ TEASPOON CLOVES

¹/₈ TEASPOON NUTMEG

¹/₄ CUP CHOPPED TOASTED PECANS

Pecan Praline Topping (recipe follows)

MAKES
one 9-inch
square cake

PREHEAT OVEN TO 350°F (175°C).

Cream sugar, butter and bananas until smooth and creamy. Beat in buttermilk, rum and egg. Blend in all remaining ingredients except topping. Pour into greased and floured 9-inch square pan. Bake 25 to 30 minutes, or until toothpick inserted in center comes out clean. Cool completely, then spread with frosting. (Note: To double recipe, use a 10 x 15-inch jelly roll pan.)

Pecan Praline Topping

1/4   CUP (1/2 stick) BUTTER OR MARGARINE

1/2   CUP FIRMLY PACKED DARK BROWN SUGAR

5   TABLESPOONS MILK

2   CUPS POWDERED SUGAR

1   TEASPOON VANILLA EXTRACT

1/2   CUP TOASTED PECAN HALVES, COARSELY BROKEN

Bring butter and sugar to boil in small saucepan. Cook over medium heat, stirring, 1 minute or until slightly thickened. Let cool 10 minutes. Beat in milk, powdered sugar and vanilla. Stir in nuts.

Note: This cake is a must at a New Orleans-style brunch. Cut into small squares and add to your bread basket. Serve with eggs Hussard, eggs Sardou or grillades and grits.

147

Lane Cake is an old Southern standby and an American classic, even referred to in the great novel To Kill a Mockingbird. *There are many versions, with various batters and fruit combinations, but basically, it's a rich golden yellow cake sandwiched with three to four layers of fruit-and-nut filling. This recipe features an interesting batter in which whipped cream acts as shortening and leavening.*

★ ★ ★

LUSCIOUS LANE CAKE

1½   CUPS CHILLED HEAVY CREAM
3   EGGS
1½   TEASPOONS VANILLA EXTRACT
2   CUPS ALL PURPOSE FLOUR
1½   CUPS SUGAR
2   TEASPOONS BAKING POWDER
½   TEASPOON SALT
     Fruit and Nut Filling (recipe follows)

MAKES
one 9-inch
layer cake

PREHEAT OVEN TO 350°F (175°C).

Beat cream until stiff and set aside. Beat eggs with vanilla until thick and fluffy. Gently fold into whipped cream. Stir dry ingredients together and fold into cream mixture. Spread into two greased and floured 9-inch round cake pans. Bake 30 to 35 minutes, until toothpick inserted in center comes out clean. Let cool in pan 10 minutes. Remove from pans and cool cakes completely on wire racks. Split each layer in half horizontally and gently spread with filling; stack layers with another layer of filling. Spread remaining filling on top of cake.

Fruit and Nut Filling

4 EGG YOLKS

1⅓ CUPS SOUR CREAM

1⅓ CUPS SUGAR

2 CUPS CHOPPED TOASTED PECANS

1 CUP GOLDEN RAISINS

1 CUP CHOPPED CANDIED CHERRIES

1 CUP CHOPPED CANDIED PINEAPPLE

1 CUP CHOPPED PITTED DATES

1 CUP SHREDDED COCONUT

1 TABLESPOON BOURBON OR RUM

Combine egg yolks, sour cream and sugar in saucepan. Blend in remaining ingredients and cook, stirring, until mixture bubbles and begins to thicken. Let cool to room temperature before spreading on cake.

This is one of those wonderful large sheet cakes to sell by the slice or bring to a barbecue. Frosting lovers will delight in the thick, rich layer of coconut cream on top. (Bite for bite, you'll get a little cake with your frosting!)

PINEAPPLE PARADISE CAKE

20-OUNCE CAN (2½ cups) CRUSHED PINEAPPLE WITH JUICE

2   CUPS ALL PURPOSE FLOUR

2   CUPS SUGAR

2   EGGS

1   TEASPOON BAKING SODA

½   CUP VEGETABLE OIL

½   TEASPOON COCONUT FLAVORING

Coconut Cream Frosting (recipe follows)

MAKES

one

10 x 15-inch

sheet cake

PREHEAT OVEN TO 350°F (175°C).

Using a fork or slotted spoon, set aside ¼ cup pineapple for frosting. Combine remaining pineapple with all ingredients except frosting in mixing bowl. Beat at medium speed 2 minutes. Pour into greased and floured 10 x 15-inch pan. Bake 20 to 25 minutes, until toothpick inserted in center comes out clean. Let cool completely, then frost.

Coconut Cream Frosting

8-OUNCE PACKAGE CREAM CHEESE, SOFTENED
$^1/_4$ CUP ($^1/_2$ stick) BUTTER OR MARGARINE, SOFTENED
$^1/_4$ CUP SOUR CREAM
1 TEASPOON VANILLA EXTRACT
$^1/_4$ TEASPOON COCONUT FLAVORING
4 CUPS (1 pound) POWDERED SUGAR
$^1/_2$ CUP SHREDDED COCONUT
$^1/_4$ CUP RESERVED PINEAPPLE

Beat cream cheese, butter, sour cream and flavorings until smooth and creamy. Add powdered sugar and beat until frosting is spreadable consistency. Stir in coconut and pineapple.

DECORATION IDEA: Score through frosting to mark 24 servings. Cut a fresh (unpeeled) pineapple into bite-size wedges (1 inch wide, $^1/_2$ inch thick). Dip one side of each pineapple piece into a little melted chocolate. Arrange in rows, in the center of each cake serving.

I came across this jewel of a cake at a bake sale in St. Joseph, Missouri. The original version features a bourbon frosting; I substituted brandy in this recipe (a personal preference). Either way, it makes a simple, sophisticated cake for company.

★ ★ ★

APRICOT BRANDY CAKE

MAKES one 8-inch layer cake

2	CUPS ALL PURPOSE FLOUR
1¾	CUPS SUGAR
1	TABLESPOON BAKING POWDER
½	TEASPOON SALT
1	CUP VEGETABLE OIL
2	4½-OUNCE JARS APRICOT BABY FOOD
3	EGGS
2	TEASPOONS VANILLA EXTRACT
1	TEASPOON CINNAMON
½	TEASPOON CLOVES
½	CUP APRICOT PRESERVES

Brandy Buttercream Frosting (recipe follows)

PREHEAT OVEN TO 350°F (175°C).

Combine flour, sugar, baking powder, salt, oil, baby food, eggs, vanilla, cinnamon, and cloves in mixing bowl and beat at medium speed for 2 minutes. Pour into two greased and floured 8-inch round pans. Bake 30 to 35 minutes, until toothpick inserted in center comes out clean. Let cool in pans.

Remove layers from pans and sandwich together with apricot preserves. Spread top and sides of cake with frosting.

Opposite: Luscious Lane Cake (background), page 148;
Red Devil Magic Mayonnaise Cake (foreground), page 134
Overleaf: Strawberry Rhubarb Cake, page 154

Luscious Lane
Cake
25¢ raffle

Red Devil
Magic Mayonnaise
Cake
25¢ raffle

Strawberry-Rhubarb
Cake
$1·10
a slice

Brandy Buttercream Frosting

3	CUPS POWDERED SUGAR
3	TABLESPOONS BUTTER OR MARGARINE, SOFTENED
2 to 3	TABLESPOONS LIGHT CREAM OR HALF AND HALF
2	TABLESPOONS BRANDY OR BOURBON

Combine all ingredients in mixing bowl and beat to spreading consistency.

Opposite: Bee Sting Buns, page 179
Overleaf: Lemon Tea Loaf, page 173

A summertime country fair favorite.

★ ★ ★

STRAWBERRY RHUBARB CAKE

2 CUPS FINELY CHOPPED FRESH RHUBARB

2 CUPS ALL PURPOSE FLOUR

1¼ CUPS SUGAR

½ CUP VEGETABLE OIL

3 EGGS

1¼ TEASPOONS BAKING SODA

½ TEASPOON SALT

1 TEASPOON CINNAMON

1 TEASPOON NUTMEG

1 TEASPOON VANILLA EXTRACT

1 CUP CHOPPED WALNUTS

Strawberry Buttercream (recipe follows)

PREHEAT OVEN TO 350°F (175°C).

Combine all ingredients except buttercream in mixing bowl and beat 2 minutes at medium speed. Pour into two greased and floured 9-inch round pans. Bake 35 to 40 minutes, until toothpick inserted in center comes out clean. Let cool 10 minutes.

Remove layers from pans and cool completely on wire racks. Fill and frost cake with strawberry buttercream.

Strawberry Buttercream

     3-OUNCE PACKAGE CREAM CHEESE, SOFTENED

$^1/_2$ CUP (1 stick) BUTTER OR MARGARINE, SOFTENED

 4   CUPS (1 pound) POWDERED SUGAR

$^1/_2$ CUP STRAWBERRY PRESERVES

Combine all ingredients in mixing bowl and beat until smooth and creamy.

155

PINEAPPLE "RIGHT-SIDE-UP" CAKES

MAKES

two 9-inch

single-layer

cakes

BATTER FOR LUSCIOUS LANE CAKE (see page 148)

$1/2$ CUP (1 stick) BUTTER OR MARGARINE, SOFTENED

$1^{1}/_{2}$ CUPS FIRMLY PACKED BROWN SUGAR

1 TABLESPOON ALL PURPOSE FLOUR

8-OUNCE CAN CRUSHED PINEAPPLE, WELL DRAINED

$3/4$ CUP CHOPPED PECANS

2 DOZEN MARASCHINO CHERRIES

PREHEAT OVEN TO 350°F (175°C).

Bake two 9-inch layers according to the recipe for Lane Cake. Do not remove cakes from pan. Cream butter with brown sugar and flour. Stir in pineapple and pecans. Spread over cakes, dividing evenly. Arrange 12 cherries around edge of each layer. Broil cakes 2 to 3 inches from heat until golden brown and bubbly.

No "New Coke," please, for this American classic. And please don't try to pull off a Pepsi swap...although, down South, I've had versions of this cake made with Dr. Pepper!

★ ★ ★

CHOCOLATE COCA-COLA CAKE

one 9 x 13-inch

sheet cake

2   CUPS ALL PURPOSE FLOUR

2   CUPS SUGAR

3   TABLESPOONS UNSWEETENED COCOA POWDER

1   TEASPOON BAKING SODA

1   CUP COCA-COLA CLASSIC®

1   CUP (2 sticks) BUTTER OR MARGARINE

1/2   CUP BUTTERMILK

2   EGGS, WELL BEATEN

1   TEASPOON VANILLA EXTRACT

2   CUPS MINIATURE MARSHMALLOWS

Coca-Cola Frosting (recipe follows)

PREHEAT OVEN TO 350°F (175°C).

Combine flour, sugar, cocoa and baking soda in mixing bowl. Combine Coca-Cola and butter in saucepan and bring to boil. Pour over dry ingredients and stir to blend. Mix in buttermilk, eggs, vanilla and marshmallows. (Batter will be thin.) Pour into greased and floured 9 x 13-inch pan. Bake 35 to 38 minutes. Let cool 15 minutes, then spread with warm frosting.

Coca-Cola Frosting

$\frac{1}{2}$ CUP (1 stick) BUTTER OR MARGARINE

6   TABLESPOONS COCA-COLA CLASSIC®

3   TABLESPOONS UNSWEETENED COCOA POWDER

4   CUPS (1 pound) POWDERED SUGAR

1   CUP CHOPPED, TOASTED PECANS

Combine butter, cola and cocoa in saucepan and bring just to boil.
Pour over powdered sugar and blend until smooth. Stir in pecans.
Use while warm.

Variation ★ ★ ★ ★ ★ ★ ★ ★ ★ ★ ★ ★ ★ ★ ★ ★

For a Dr. Pepper cake allow a can of regular (not diet) Dr. Pepper to
go flat. Substitute Dr. Pepper for Coca-Cola Classic® in batter and
frosting.

Fans of Reese's® peanut butter cups freak out when these show up at a bake sale. (I know; I've personally walked away with a dozen). This batter is a snap: Just mix in a blender or food processor.

★ ★ ★

PEANUT BUTTER CUPCAKES

MAKES

1½ dozen

1¼	CUPS ALL PURPOSE FLOUR
1	CUP FIRMLY PACKED LIGHT BROWN SUGAR
¾	CUP MILK
¼	CUP PEANUT BUTTER
1	EGG
1	TABLESPOON BUTTER OR MARGARINE, SOFTENED
1	TABLESPOON VEGETABLE OIL
1	TEASPOON VANILLA EXTRACT
1½	TEASPOONS BAKING POWDER
½	TEASPOON SALT
½	CUP SEMISWEET CHOCOLATE CHIPS
	Peanut Butter Frosting (recipe follows)
⅔	CUP CHOPPED HONEY-ROASTED PEANUTS (optional)

PREHEAT OVEN TO 350°F (175°C).

Combine all ingredients except frosting and peanuts in blender. Cover and blend at high speed about 45 seconds, stopping motor once or twice to scrape down sides. Pour into muffin tins fitted with paper cupcake liners, filling each about ⅔ full. Bake 25 to 30 minutes, until toothpick inserted in center comes out clean. Cool cupcakes completely. Spread with frosting. If desired, garnish with chopped honey-roasted peanuts.

Peanut Butter Frosting

3 CUPS POWDERED SUGAR

$^{1}/_{4}$ CUP ($^{1}/_{2}$ stick) BUTTER OR MARGARINE, SOFTENED

$^{1}/_{4}$ CUP PEANUT BUTTER

1 TEASPOON VANILLA EXTRACT

2 TABLESPOONS MILK

Combine all ingredients in bowl and beat to a smooth, spreadable consistency.

Variation ★ ★ ★ ★ ★ ★ ★ ★ ★ ★ ★ ★ ★ ★ ★ ★ ★

For "peanut butter fudge" frosting, add $^{1}/_{4}$ cup cocoa to frosting. Increase milk to 3 tablespoons.

FRUITCAKE CUPS

MAKES
6 dozen

¹/₂ CUP (1 stick) BUTTER OR MARGARINE, SOFTENED

³/₄ CUP FIRMLY PACKED BROWN SUGAR

1   EGG

2   TABLESPOONS BOURBON OR ORANGE LIQUEUR

1¹/₂ CUPS ALL PURPOSE FLOUR

¹/₂ TEASPOON BAKING SODA

¹/₂ CUP GOLDEN RAISINS

¹/₂ CUP CHOPPED FIGS

¹/₂ CUP CHOPPED CANDIED PINEAPPLE

¹/₂ CUP CHOPPED CANDIED CHERRIES

1   CUP TOASTED PECAN HALVES, COARSELY BROKEN

PREHEAT OVEN TO 375°F (190°C).

Cream butter with sugar until smooth. Beat in egg and bourbon. Blend in dry ingredients and stir in fruits and pecans. Spoon into miniature muffin tins fitted with petite cupcake liners. Bake 9 minutes. Let cool.

161

These chewy-crusted cupcakes will remind you of coconut macaroons. For an interesting touch, try brushing tops with a light layer of apricot glaze.

★ ★ ★

COCOROON CAKES

$^3/_4$ CUP ALL PURPOSE FLOUR

$1^1/_3$ CUPS SUGAR

$1^1/_2$ CUPS ($3^1/_2$-ounce can) COCONUT

$^1/_2$ TEASPOON BAKING POWDER

$^1/_4$ TEASPOON SALT

6 EGG WHITES

$^1/_2$ TEASPOON CREAM OF TARTAR

1 TEASPOON ALMOND EXTRACT

Apricot Glaze (recipe follows)

MAKES

$1^1/_2$ dozen

PREHEAT OVEN TO 350°F (175°C).

Combine flour, 1 cup sugar, coconut, baking powder and salt in medium bowl. Stir to blend and set aside. In bowl of electric mixer, beat egg whites with cream of tartar and almond extract until foamy. Gradually add remaining $^1/_3$ cup sugar, beating until stiff peaks form. Gently fold flour mixture into egg whites. Spoon batter into muffin cups fitted with paper liners, filling about $^2/_3$ full. Bake 25 to 30 minutes, until tops are golden brown and dry. Let cool completely. If desired, brush with warm apricot glaze. Omit glaze if serving at a Fourth of July "berry bash." See note on next page.

Apricot Glaze

12-OUNCE JAR APRICOT PRESERVES

Strain preserves through sieve. Bring to boil in small saucepan (or in microwave), then let cool about 15 minutes.

Note: Strawberry shortcake is synonymous with summertime, fireworks, and the Fourth of July. For added spark, why not try red, white, and blueberry Cocoroon Cakes! Sweetened fresh strawberries and blueberries teamed with a cream cheese "creme fraiche," make a patriotic presentation. Remove cupcake liners and invert cakes in serving dishes. Arrange bowls of strawberries and blueberries with a bowl of the following topping, and let the crowd create their own bang up dessert.

Cream Cheese "Creme Fraiche"

4   8-OUNCE PACKAGES SOFTENED CREAM CHEESE
2   CUPS POWDERED SUGAR
    JUICE AND GRATED PEEL OF 1 LEMON
2   TEASPOONS VANILLA EXTRACT
1   PINT SOUR CREAM

Beat cream cheese and powdered sugar until smooth. Blend in lemon juice, peel, and vanilla. Stir in sour cream. Chill until serving. This is enough for 36 Cocoroon Cakes.

These applesauce cupcakes resemble old-fashioned caramel apples on a stick.

★ ★ ★

COUNTRY FAIR CARAMEL APPLE CAKES

1²/₃	CUPS ALL PURPOSE FLOUR
1	CUP FIRMLY PACKED LIGHT BROWN SUGAR
1	TEASPOON CINNAMON
¹/₂	TEASPOON ALLSPICE
1	TEASPOON BAKING SODA
¹/₂	TEASPOON SALT
³/₄	CUP APPLESAUCE
¹/₄	CUP SOUR CREAM
¹/₃	CUP VEGETABLE OIL
1	TABLESPOON LEMON JUICE
	CARAMEL GLAZE (recipe follows)
¹/₂	CUP CHOPPED TOASTED WALNUTS
12	POPSICLE STICKS

MAKES
1 dozen

PREHEAT OVEN TO 350°F (175°C).

Combine flour, sugar, spices, soda and salt in mixing bowl. Stir in applesauce, sour cream, oil and lemon juice. Pour into muffin tins fitted with paper liners. Bake 20 minutes. Let cool completely on wire rack.

Spread caramel glaze over tops of cupcakes and insert stick upright in center of each. Garnish rim of each cake with chopped walnuts to resemble caramel apples dipped in nuts.

Caramel Glaze

20 CARAMELS
 3 TABLESPOONS MILK

Melt caramels with milk in small saucepan over low heat, stirring until smooth.

Note: For a festive touch, I like to cut 6 inch lengths of red gingham ribbon and tie bows on each stick.

THE TOP TEN BREADWINNERS

"SALAD BAR BREAD"
(Classic Carrot, Zucchini and Waldorf Apple)

LEMON TEA LOAF

CABANA BANANA BREAD

INDIAN PUMPKIN BREAD

CAPE COD CRANBERRY CORNBREAD

BENNINGTON BLUEBERRY MAPLE MUFFINS

BEE STING BUNS

QUICK STICKY "SINNABUNS"

COTTAGE HERB GARDEN BREAD

TAVERN CHEDDAR CHEESE BREAD

TOP TEN BREADWINNERS

No one can resist a freshly baked loaf of bread, so the bread table is always a big attraction at bake sales. Whether you're bringing the loaves or buying them, they freeze well and make great all-purpose gifts. (My favorite purpose is to give one to myself!)

The following collection contains some of the most popular breads found at bake sales (including some interesting variations that I've encountered). It's no surprise that everyone's favorite breads to bring are also the easiest breads to bake!

"BREAD BEEFS"

This is a collection of bread recipes for those of you who hate being held in bondage by yeast. You yeast slaves know what I'm talking about. The dough never rises while you're watching it, so you leave the room. But if you go away for too long, it climbs up out of the bowl and takes over the kitchen, just like an episode out of "I Love Lucy." I hate scraping dough off the floor.

But some people actually enjoy babysitting bread; it gives them a nurturing feeling. For them I've included one-step, single-rise bread recipes. If you're the impatient type (like me), don't torture yourself. Try baking batter breads and shortcut rolls.

Salad bar breads can be made by taking a simple trip to your supermarket deli department. Quick sticky "Sinnabuns" are almost as fast as opening a can of caramel rolls (and far more gratifying) and if opening a can is about all that you're up to, be creative with Bee Sting Buns. Refrigerated crescent rolls make these a snap. And you thought you were too busy to bake bread!

(Classic Carrot, Zucchini, Waldorf Apple, Broccoli, and Pepper Relish)

Tea breads made with grated carrots, zucchini or apples are a bake sale tradition. With the common ingredient of mayonnaise binding these breads together, you could easily bake up a batch after a visit to the supermarket salad bar!

★ ★ ★

"SALAD BAR BREAD"

BASIC BATTER (CLASSIC CARROT BREAD):

2½	CUPS ALL PURPOSE FLOUR
3	EGGS, LIGHTLY BEATEN
1	CUP REAL MAYONNAISE OR SALAD DRESSING
1	CUP SUGAR
2	CUPS GRATED CARROTS
2	TEASPOONS VANILLA EXTRACT
1	TEASPOON BAKING POWDER
1	TEASPOON BAKING SODA
1	TABLESPOON CINNAMON
1	TEASPOON SALT
⅔	CUP RAISINS
1	CUP CHOPPED TOASTED PECANS OR WALNUTS

MAKES
two 9 x 5-inch
loaves

PREHEAT OVEN TO 350°F (175°C).

Blend all ingredients in mixing bowl until thoroughly combined. Divide batter between two greased 9 x 5-inch loaf pans. Bake 1 hour. Let cool 10 minutes, then remove from pans (or, if using foil loaf pans, leave bread in pan).

ZUCCHINI BREAD: Substitute 2 cups grated, drained zucchini for carrots.

171

WALDORF APPLE BREAD: Substitute 1½ cups grated apples (drained), and ½ cup finely chopped celery for carrots.

BROCCOLI BREAD: Substitute 1½ cups chopped fresh broccoli (tops only) and ½ cup chopped celery for carrots. Substitute 1 cup toasted almonds for walnuts. Omit cinnamon and raisins.

PEPPER RELISH BREAD: Substitute 1 cup cooked yellow kernel corn, ½ cup chopped red bell pepper, and ½ cup chopped green bell pepper, for carrots. Substitute ½ cup chopped celery for raisins. Add 2 tablespoons sweet pickle relish.

A luscious, refreshing tea loaf that doubles as a dessert cake. The glaze makes it extra moist.

★ ★ ★

LEMON TEA LOAF

1/2	CUP (1 stick) BUTTER OR MARGARINE, SOFTENED
1 1/2	CUPS SUGAR
4	EGGS
2	TABLESPOONS GRATED LEMON PEEL
1	TABLESPOON LEMON EXTRACT
4	TEASPOONS BAKING POWDER
1	TEASPOON SALT
1 1/2	CUPS LIGHT CREAM
2	CUPS ALL PURPOSE FLOUR
1	CUP CHOPPED TOASTED ALMONDS
1/3	CUP SUGAR
1/4	CUP LEMON JUICE

MAKES two 9 x 5-inch loaves

PREHEAT OVEN TO 350°F (175°C).

Cream butter with 1 1/2 cups sugar until very light and fluffy. Add eggs one at a time and beat at high speed of electric mixer 3 to 5 minutes. Beat in grated peel, lemon extract, baking powder and salt. At low speed, gently mix in cream and flour alternately until blended. Stir in almonds. Divide batter between two greased 9 x 5-inch loaf pans. Bake 50 to 55 minutes.

Meanwhile, combine ⅓ cup sugar with lemon juice. Spoon glaze slowly over hot loaves, allowing it to soak in. Cool loaves about 30 minutes, then gently remove from pans (or, if using foil loaf pans, leave bread in pan).

Note: my favorite presentation of this popular bake sale item is to package loaves in "lemon bags." To make lemon bags, purchase white paper bakery sacks from a paper outlet. (Or you can also use traditional brown lunch bags.) Slice lemons in half and allow them to dry out overnight. Print bags with lemons dipped, cut side down, in yellow paint. (It's just like making a potato print.) When bags are dry, slide leaves in and seal with a gold sticker.

Banana bread with a tropical twist of pineapple and coconut.

★ ★ ★

CABANA BANANA BREAD

MAKES
two 9 x 5-inch
loaves

1/2 CUP (1 stick) BUTTER OR MARGARINE, SOFTENED

2 CUPS FIRMLY PACKED LIGHT BROWN SUGAR

4 MEDIUM-SIZE RIPE BANANAS

4 EGGS

1/2 CUP VEGETABLE OIL

1 CUP SWISS-STYLE PINEAPPLE YOGURT

1/2 CUP CRUSHED PINEAPPLE, VERY WELL DRAINED

1 TEASPOON VANILLA EXTRACT

1/2 TEASPOON COCONUT EXTRACT

3 CUPS ALL PURPOSE FLOUR

2 TEASPOONS BAKING SODA

1/2 TEASPOON SALT

1/2 CUP SHREDDED COCONUT

PREHEAT OVEN TO 350°F (175°C).

Cream butter and sugar until light and fluffy. Beat in bananas until mashed and smooth. Beat in eggs one at a time. Blend in oil. Mix in all remaining ingredients except coconut. Divide batter between two greased 9 x 5-inch loaf pans. Sprinkle coconut evenly over tops of loaves. Bake 50 to 60 minutes, until toothpick inserted in center comes out clean. Let cool 5 minutes before removing from pans (or, if using foil loaf pans, leave bread in pan).

I came across this version at a bake sale in Woonsocket, Rhode Island. I'm completely sold on it as the ultimate pumpkin bread. The cornmeal adds interesting character.

★ ★ ★

INDIAN PUMPKIN BREAD

1	CUP SUGAR
1	CUP FIRMLY PACKED BROWN SUGAR
1	CUP VEGETABLE OIL
3	EGGS
2	CUPS CANNED PUMPKIN
2	CUPS ALL PURPOSE FLOUR
1	CUP WHITE OR YELLOW CORNMEAL
$\frac{1}{2}$	TEASPOON SALT
$\frac{1}{2}$	TEASPOON BAKING POWDER
1	TEASPOON BAKING SODA
1	TEASPOON CLOVES
1	TEASPOON CINNAMON
$\frac{2}{3}$	CUP RAISINS
$\frac{2}{3}$	CUP CHOPPED TOASTED WALNUTS

MAKES

two 9 x 5-inch

loaves

PREHEAT OVEN TO 325°F (160°C).

In large mixing bowl, blend sugars and oil. Add egg and beat until light and fluffy. Blend in pumpkin. Combine dry ingredients and blend into pumpkin mixture. Stir in raisins and walnuts. Divide between two greased and floured 9 x 5-inch loaf pans. Bake 65 to 70 minutes, until toothpick inserted in center comes out clean. Let cool 10 minutes before removing from pans.

A delicious addition to a holiday menu featuring roast turkey or baked ham. Or try it for breakfast with butter and hot maple syrup.

★ ★ ★

CAPE COD CRANBERRY CORNBREAD

1	CUP YELLOW CORNMEAL
1	CUP ALL PURPOSE FLOUR
$1/2$	CUP FIRMLY PACKED LIGHT BROWN SUGAR
1	CUP BUTTERMILK
6	TABLESPOONS (3/4 stick) MELTED BUTTER OR MARGARINE
1	EGG, SLIGHTLY BEATEN
$2^1/2$	TEASPOONS BAKING POWDER
$1/4$	TEASPOON SALT
1	CUP FRESH CRANBERRIES, COARSELY CHOPPED
1	CUP CHOPPED WALNUTS

MAKES
9 squares

PREHEAT OVEN TO 400°F (200°C).

Gently blend all ingredients except walnuts in mixing bowl with fork or rubber spatula. Spread into greased 9-inch square pan. Sprinkle with walnuts. Bake 25 minutes, until toothpick inserted in center comes out clean. Serve warm.

Blueberries, bran cereal and maple syrup team up to create a "very Vermont" muffin.

★ ★ ★

BENNINGTON BLUEBERRY MAPLE MUFFINS

MAKES
1½ dozen

1	CUP LIGHTLY CRUSHED BRAN FLAKES
1	CUP SOUR CREAM
1	CUP MAPLE SYRUP
2	EGGS
2	CUPS ALL PURPOSE FLOUR
2	TEASPOONS BAKING SODA
1	CUP BLUEBERRIES
1	CUP CHOPPED WALNUTS

PREHEAT OVEN TO 400°F (200°C).

The night before baking, combine bran flakes with sour cream and maple syrup. Refrigerate overnight. Beat eggs until frothy and blend into bran flake mixture. Combine flour with baking soda and stir into batter until blended (be careful not to overmix). Fold in blueberries. Spoon batter into 18 greased or paper-lined muffin cups. Sprinkle walnuts evenly over muffins. Bake 15 to 20 minutes. Let cool 5 minutes, then remove muffins from tins.

For those bread bakers who want "instant gratification," this is it! The hard part comes in a can, and the rest is a snap. These gooey, golden sweet rolls come out looking very sophisticated.

★ ★ ★

BEE STING BUNS

MAKES
16 buns

2   8-OUNCE CANS REFRIGERATED CRESCENT ROLLS
    8-OUNCE PACKAGE CREAM CHEESE
¼   CUP (½ stick) MELTED BUTTER OR MARGARINE
¼   CUP FIRMLY PACKED LIGHT BROWN SUGAR
3   TABLESPOONS HONEY
1   TEASPOON GRATED ORANGE PEEL
½   TEASPOON ALMOND EXTRACT
⅔   CUP SLIVERED ALMONDS

PREHEAT OVEN TO 375°F (190°C).

Unroll crescents and divide into scored triangles. Cut cream cheese block into 16 cubes. Place one cube at base of each triangle and roll up to enclose cheese. Bring ends of crescents together, forming balls.

Spray 16 muffin cups with nonstick coating. Combine remaining ingredients and spoon into bottoms of muffin cups. Place ball of dough in each cup. Bake 15 to 20 minutes, until golden brown and bubbly. Let cool 1 minute, then immediately invert onto foil.

179

Sinfully rich, good and gooey—sticky buns without the wait. These are based on a cinnamon buttermilk biscuit dough, so there's no waiting for the buns to rise.

★ ★ ★

QUICK STICKY "SINNABUNS"

MAKES
1 dozen

2 CUPS ALL PURPOSE FLOUR

¼ CUP FIRMLY PACKED LIGHT BROWN SUGAR

1 TEASPOON CINNAMON

¼ TEASPOON BAKING SODA

1 TABLESPOON BAKING POWDER

½ TEASPOON SALT

⅓ CUP BUTTER OR MARGARINE

½ CUP BUTTERMILK

1 EGG

Filling (recipe follows)

Glaze (recipe follows)

½ CUP CHOPPED PECANS

PREHEAT OVEN TO 400°F (200°C).

Combine flour, brown sugar, cinnamon, soda, baking powder and salt in mixing bowl. Stir with fork to blend. Using pastry blender, cut butter into dry mixture to resemble coarse crumbs. Beat buttermilk with egg in measuring cup and pour into bowl. Stir with fork until dough forms ball. Turn dough out on lightly floured surface and knead about 5 times, until no longer sticky. Pat dough into 12 x 8-inch rectangle. Spread with filling and roll up into 12-inch-long "jelly roll." Cut into 1-inch-thick slices.

Spray 9 x 13-inch pan with nonstick coating. Spread glaze in bottom and sprinkle evenly with pecans. Arrange rolls in four rows on top of glaze. Bake 15 to 20 minutes, until rolls are golden and glaze is bubbly (don't overbake; these burn easily). Let cool 1 minute, then immediately invert onto sheet of waxed paper or foil.

Filling

3 TABLESPOONS BUTTER OR MARGARINE, SOFTENED
1/2 CUP FIRMLY PACKED LIGHT BROWN SUGAR
2 TEASPOONS CINNAMON

Blend all ingredients until smooth.

Glaze

1/2 CUP (1 stick) BUTTER OR MARGARINE
1/2 CUP FIRMLY PACKED BROWN SUGAR
3 TABLESPOONS HONEY

Combine all ingredients in saucepan and stir over low heat until well blended.

This homey herb batter bread is classically made with cottage cheese and baked in casseroles. Try it toasted!

★ ★ ★

COTTAGE HERB GARDEN BREAD

4½	CUPS ALL PURPOSE FLOUR
2	TABLESPOONS SUGAR
2	ENVELOPES DRY YEAST
1	ENVELOPE (1 ounce/30 g) RANCH-STYLE SALAD DRESSING MIX
½	TEASPOON DRIED THYME LEAVES
1	TEASPOON PARSLEY FLAKES
1	TEASPOON DRIED DILLWEED
¾	CUP VERY HOT TAP WATER (120°F–130°F/50°C–55°C)
2	TABLESPOONS OLIVE OIL
2	EGGS, BEATEN (ROOM TEMPERATURE)
1	CUP CHIVE-FLAVORED COTTAGE CHEESE (ROOM TEMPERATURE)
⅓	CUP GRATED PARMESAN CHEESE

MAKES
2 loaves

Combine dry ingredients in mixing bowl. Stir in hot water. Add eggs and cheeses and blend well (dough will be soft and sticky). Cover bowl with towel and let dough rise until doubled.

Punch dough down. Divide between two well-greased 1-quart casseroles. Cover and let rise until doubled, about 1 hour.

PREHEAT OVEN TO 375°F (190°C).

Bake loaves for 35 minutes, until golden brown. Let cool 10 minutes, then remove from casseroles and cool completely on wire racks.

A hearty beer batter bread with bacon bits and sharp aged cheddar cheese.

★ ★ ★

TAVERN CHEDDAR CHEESE BREAD

MAKES
one 9 x 5-inch
loaf

³/₄ CUP WARM, FLAT BEER (105°F–115°F/40°C–45°C)

1 ENVELOPE DRY YEAST

1 EGG, BEATEN

¹/₄ CUP SUGAR

¹/₄ CUP OLIVE OIL

³/₄ CUP PEELED, SEEDED AND CHOPPED RIPE TOMATO

³/₄ CUP GRATED AGED CHEDDAR CHEESE SUCH AS OLD ENGLISH

4 STRIPS BACON, COOKED EXTRA-CRISP AND CRUMBLED

3¹/₂ CUPS ALL PURPOSE FLOUR

Combine beer and yeast in mixing bowl and let stand until yeast is dissolved. Add all remaining ingredients and blend well. Pour into greased 9 x 5-inch loaf pan. Cover with towel and let rise until doubled, about 1 hour.

PREHEAT OVEN TO 350°F (175°C).

Bake 30 minutes. Let cool 10 minutes, then remove from pan and cool on wire rack.

"IT'S A WRAP"

Packaging helps sell a product or enhance the presentation of a gift. Even though the charm of home baked goods is, well, their homeliness, there are times when it's appropriate to incorporate some professional marketing techniques.

Schools, churches, hospitals and other charitable institutions can raise a lot of revenue during holiday seasons by packaging their goodies as appealing gift items. You can use the same ideas to take care of everyone on your Christmas list. The following suggestions are just a sampling of the possibilities.

STICKERS AND LABELS:

You don't need a printing press to enhance a package with your organization's logo or your own personal label. Go to a stationery store, where you can buy simple string tags in decorator colors to match ribbons, bags and tissue. Pressure-sensitive label paper can actually be run through a copier machine; this allows you to transfer dozens of emblems and logos from any ordinary letterhead—or custom sketch—effortlessly. You can then cut the labels apart with a paper cutter.

Rubber stamps can be used on cards or paper bags with an attractive array of ink colors. And my personal favorite? Notary seals. These beautiful gold badges make everything look elegant. You can easily imprint them with an embosser, using a standard plate of changeable letters (like school initials…or your own initials). You might want to have a custom plate made up for your organization or yourself (mine says, "From the Kitchen of AMB").

PANS:

The simplest package of all is a self-contained aluminum baking pan with a plastic cover. (These are especially nice for cakes or bars because you never have to transfer them out of the pan to package them.) These containers are commonly found at paper-supply outlets...or at the salad bar of your local supermarket! (Many stores will donate them for a community cause or charity.) Dress them up with a nice sticker and a streamer of ribbon.

BOXES:

These, too, are available at paper-supply outlets—or you can buy gift boxes at stationery shops for a higher price. It really depends on what quantity you need. Buying in bulk only makes sense if you won't be stuck with hundreds of leftover boxes. One of my favorite boxes for cookies is a Chinese restaurant carry-out container. These come in many sizes, and are inexpensive and easily customized. Try rubber-stamping, or running a ribbon around the box and securing it with a seal.

BAGS:

These are great for cookies and breads. White bakery bags (even brown lunch bags) can be pinked at the open edge, folded over and sealed with a sticker. (My favorite presentation of lemon bread is to slip it into a bag that has been stamped with yellow "lemon slices"...just like a potato print.) Plastic quart-size bags also work well for bread. These can be gathered at the open end and tied with a cord or bow. Don't overlook coffee bags with twist-down tops …very effective for cookies.

CELLOPHANE, TISSUES:

Cellophane has long been recognized as an attractive way to view what you get. Just be sure the cellophane you buy is approved for use on food, fruits and vegetables. Bless the plastic-wrap people for the brainstorm of colored cling wraps! Now you can seal in freshness and add a professional touch to baked goods with a simple supermarket product. Tissue paper can also be wrapped around cookies or bread when lined with a layer of plastic wrap.

I like to create what I call a "carnation bag." Gather all the ends together and tie off in a pompom. Then cut straight across the pompom with pinking shears. Spread with your fingers and voilà— a carnation.

BASKETS:

Gift baskets are the ultimate extravagance, and need not be reserved for Easter. They are nice to use when combining several types of products into a gift assortment. Basket "grass" runs the gamut of colors, making a perfect nest for goodies. For a dramatic touch, wrap the baskets in a sheet of shimmering iridescent cellophane. Not all baskets need be a big investment; in fact, my favorite are strawberry crates and cherry tomato cartons.

Anything goes. As long as there's imagination, there's inspiration …experiment! Who knows what wonders you might work with a batch of brownies and a paint bucket?

BAKING MEASUREMENTS

Here are some general kitchen measurements which may be of help in your baking.
These measurements are for U.S. cooks.

3 teaspoons = 1 tablespoon
4 tablespoons = $\frac{1}{4}$ cup
$5\frac{1}{3}$ tablespoons = $\frac{1}{3}$ cup
8 tablespoons = $\frac{1}{2}$ cup

1 cup = $\frac{1}{2}$ pint or 8 fluid ounces
2 cups = 1 pint or 16 fluid ounces
1 quart (liquid) = 2 pints or 4 cups
1 gallon (liquid) = 4 quarts

5 whole eggs = 1 cup
8 to 10 egg whites = 1 cup
10 to 12 egg yolks = 1 cup

8 tablespoons butter = $\frac{1}{2}$ cup or 1 stick
2 sticks butter = 1 cup
2 cups butter = 1 pound

3 packages active dry yeast = 1 cake yeast
1 package active dry yeast = 1 scant tablespoon

1 square chocolate = 1 ounce or 1 tablespoon melted
1 ounce unsweetened chocolate = $\frac{1}{3}$ cup cocoa powder

1 pound apples = 3 cups peeled, cored, and sliced
6 ounces raisins = 1 cup
$\frac{1}{4}$ pound walnuts will yield 1 cup shelled
1 pound walnuts will yield $\frac{1}{2}$ pound shelled

1 lemon yields $2\frac{1}{2}$ to $3\frac{1}{2}$ tablespoons juice
1 orange yields 5 to 6 tablespoons juice

12 ounces honey = 1 cup
1 pound confectioners' sugar = $3\frac{1}{2}$ cups
1 pound brown sugar = $2\frac{1}{4}$ cups
1 pound granulated sugar = 2 cups

1 pound flour = approximately 4 cups
1 pound cake flour = $4\frac{1}{2}$ cups
1 pound whole wheat flour = $3\frac{3}{4}$ cups

CONVERSION TABLES

Outside the U.S., cooks measure more items by weight.
Here are approximate equivalents for basic items in this book.

	U.S. CUSTOMARY	METRIC	IMPERIAL
Apples (peeled and chopped)	2 cups	225 g	8 ounces
Butter	1 cup	225 g	8 ounces
	1/2 cup	115 g	4 ounces
	1/4 cup	60 g	2 ounces
	1 tablespoon	15 g	1/2 ounce
Chocolate chips	1/2 cup	85 g	3 ounces
Coconut (shredded)	1/2 cup	60 g	2 ounces
Flour (all purpose)	1 cup	150 g	5 ounces
Fruit (chopped)	1 cup	225 g	8 ounces
Nut Meats (chopped)	1 cup	115 g	4 ounces
Raisins (and other dried fruits)	1 cup	175 g	6 ounces
Sugar (granulated) or	1 cup	190 g	6 1/2 ounces
	1/2 cup	85 g	3 ounces
	1/4 cup	40 g	1 3/4 ounces
caster (confectioners')	1 cup	80 g	2 2/3 ounces
or icing	1/2 cup	40 g	1 1/3 ounces
	1/4 cup	20 g	3/4 ounce
brown	1 cup	160 g	5 1/3 ounces

OVEN TEMPERATURES

Fahrenheit	225	300	350	400	450
Celsius	110	150	180	200	230
Gas Mark	1/4	2	4	6	8

EMERGENCY SUBSTITUTIONS

IF YOU DON'T HAVE	SUBSTITUTE
1 cup cake flour	1 cup minus 2 tablespoons all-purpose flour
1 tablespoon cornstarch (for thickening)	2 tablespoons all purpose flour
1 teaspoon baking powder	$\frac{1}{4}$ teaspoon baking soda plus $\frac{1}{2}$ cup buttermilk or sour milk (to replace $\frac{1}{2}$ cup of the liquid called for in the recipe)
1 package active dry yeast	1 cake compressed yeast
1 cup granulated sugar	1 cup packed brown sugar or 2 cups sifted powdered sugar
1 cup honey	$1\frac{1}{4}$ cups granulated sugar plus $\frac{1}{2}$ cup water
1 square (1 ounce) unsweetened chocolate	3 tablespoons unsweetened cocoa powder plus 1 tablespoon margarine or butter
1 cup buttermilk	1 tablespoon lemon juice or vinegar plus whole milk to make 1 cup. Let stand 5 minutes before using.
1 cup whole milk	$\frac{1}{2}$ cup evaporated milk plus $\frac{1}{2}$ cup water or 1 cup reconstituted nonfat dry milk plus $2\frac{1}{2}$ teaspoons margarine or butter
1 cup half-and-half	1 cup minus 2 tablespoons whole milk plus 2 tablespoons margarine or butter
1 teaspoon finely grated lemon peel	$\frac{1}{2}$ teaspoon lemon extract

INDEX

B

C

F

Fillings. *See* Toppings and fillings

Frosting:
    almond cheese, 39
    brandy buttercream, 153
    broiled, 137
    Coca-Cola, 158
    coconut cream, 151
    coconut pecan, 135
    colonial orange, 141
    cream cheese, 129
    devil's food fudge, 135
    lemon cheese, 45
    maple butter, 143
    peanut butter, 160
    strawberry buttercream, 155
    white gold, 131

G

Glazes:
    apricot, 163
    caramel, 165
    caramel butter, 170
    chocolate, 36, 39, 133
    cranberry, 60
    lemon, 145
    orange, 43
    penuche, 85